# One of the Lads

2.2.

# One of the Lads

Anne Coddington

📖 HarperCollins*Publishers*

HarperCollins*Publishers*
77–85 Fulham Palace Road,
Hammersmith, London W6 8JB

Published by HarperCollins*Publishers* 1997

1 2 3 4 5 6 7 8 9 10

© Anne Coddington

Anne Coddington asserts the moral right to
be identified as the author of this work.

A catalogue record for this book
is available from the British Library.

ISBN 0 04 440969 9

Printed in Great Britain by
Caledonian International Book Manufacturing Ltd, Glasgow

# Contents

# Acknowledgements

Thanks to all the women fans, journalists, administrators, backroom staff, wives, mothers and daughters who are quoted in this book. I could not have written this book without you. And thanks to the women who offered support, help and important insights along the way: Jane Ashworth, Val Jones, Margaret Whisker, Sarah Parker, Janet Williamson, Yvonne Fletcher, Sheila Marson, Betty Scurr, Anna Merriman, Heidi Bell, Barbara Williams, Deidrie Barlow, Ann-Jane Wilcox, Joan and Shona Brennan, Sue Crawley, Ann and Jean Jackson, Gillian Howarth, Kath Knott, Irene Gilison, Kathryn Willgress, Sonita Alleyne, Denise Searle, Rachael Heyhoe Flint, Malcolm and Lorraine Abbott, Candice Waller, Diane Davison, Lou Waller, Kate Greenwood and all the players at Phoenix LFC.

I owe a massive debt of gratitude to all those people who provided information, articles and contacts: Adam Brown, Timothy Pinto, Philip Cornwall, Brian Spurell, Colin Jose, Pete May, Mark Sudbury, Richard Giulianotti, Oriane Baile de Laperriere, Jay Hall, Kevin Monks, Yvonne Roberts, Stephen Parrot and all the students on the 1995 Birkbeck College 'Football, Culture and Society' course.

I am especially grateful to Gail Newsham for introducing me to
Joan Whalley and driving me to Carnforth to meet her; to David Bull
for contacts in the Southampton area and introducing me to Jean
Thomasson, whose poem first appeared in Dave's edited collection
*We'll Support You Ever More*; and to Rogan Taylor for putting me
in contact with Jess Paisley, Norah Mercer and Phyllis Liddell.

Thanks to John Williams, Steve Redhead, Garry Whannel and Jonathan
Rutherford for sharing their ideas on football and masculinity with me.
Their insights have provided a context that has both shaped this book
and made the writing of it easier. All quotations from these writers are
via interview unless otherwise stated.

Sara Dunn, Belinda Budge and Christina Digby at HarperCollins
have helped me in numerous ways to write a far better book than I
could have done alone. And I thank them for their infinite patience.
Charlie Connelley also undertook additional research to check that
all my football references were factually correct.

Sitting in the West Stand Lower Tier of Tottenham's White Hart Lane
during the writing of this book hasn't unfortunately been the most
inspiring of times. But hope springs eternal and so thanks to Spurs.

Thanks also to Bernard Periatambee who during the writing of this
book was my lifeline to the outside world; he has been as always a
firm and solid friend. And to my partner Mark Perryman I am forever
grateful – if anyone has lived through this book he has. Not only did
he help me come up with the original idea which on occasion I have
been tireless in reminding him – the words 'you got me into this

mess' spring to mind – but he has been a constant source of love, encouragement and support throughout. I am particularly grateful to him for sharing with me his ideas on the modernization of football used in the conclusion.

# Introduction

Football is undergoing a sexual revolution. The near monopoly that men once had on Britain's national game is finally beginning to break up. The statistics speak for themselves: one in eight fans at Premier League games is a woman; and of the fans who started going to football since the advent of all seater stadia six years ago, women represent one in four. It doesn't end there. Ever increasing numbers of women are working within the institutions of football. They are reporting on the game for national newspapers, magazines, TV stations and national radio. In addition, over the past few years women's football has grown astronomically – over 21,000 players are now registered with the Football Association, making women's football one of the fastest growing team sports in Britain.

How did this female love affair with football come about? It was Italia 90 that heralded a new dawn for women. Whereas once football seemed in the eyes of many of us a grubby, dirty, battle-soaked game, with jeering men and incidents of violence, Italia 90 told a quite different story. Here on national TV was an aesthetically pleasing spectacle: Pavarotti singing 'Nessun Dorma', which epitomized all the passion and drama of this national footballing event; Gazza's tears represented the fragile side of this most cheeky-chappie of characters. Even the English team record for Italia 90 – performed by New Order – suggested a new openness and accessibility: it was dance music, played in clubs and pubs rather than simply a terrace dirge. Italia 90 showed a side of football that many women had never seen before: they were hooked. As theatre director and Spurs supporter Abigail Morris puts it: 'I loved the whole sense of national purpose, that you could look out of the window and see the streets deserted and know that everyone was watching the game. You felt the nation was for once unified.' Arsenal fan and TV researcher Sonia Sallas describes it thus: 'I never realized football could be so beautiful, that the movements could have such grace. I always thought of men with muddy thighs kicking a ball around a rain-soaked pitch. After Italia 90 I looked at football in a completely different way – I couldn't wait to go to a game.'

Italia 90 also happened to coincide with the transformation that was already shaking up the game domestically. In the 1970s and 80s, football was perceived as a haven for racist, sexist thugs. Sue Wallis, co-editor of the Manchester City fanzine *King of the Kippax*, a supporter during this period, remarks: 'You felt you shouldn't tell people you were a fan because they'd look at you in disgust.' Barred from European games for the hooligan activity of its fans, English football was in the doldrums. But ironically, out of one of the greatest tragedies ever to hit English football, came change. In 1989, 96 people were killed in the Hillsborough stadium disaster. The way that dreadful calamity was reported by a predominantly sympathetic media – the singular exception being

**2**

the *Sun* – was significant in changing the way football fans were perceived. As John Williams, senior researcher at the Sir Norman Chester Centre for Football Research says: 'The people involved emerged as ordinary people with jobs, families and homes. It was written up in the press in terms of the lexicon of the family: the football family had suffered a loss. No longer were spectators talked about in terms of the prism of hooliganism.' With the Taylor Report, commissioned to investigate the disaster, football was to be irrevocably changed: first by the enforced introduction of all-seater stadia in the premiership clubs, with the other divisions to follow on in quick time; and second, by a rapid process of commercialization to help fund the building work – the swapping of terraces for seats demanded. Through force of circumstance football was gearing itself up to attract new audiences. But this was not a conscious attempt to woo women. That women were being galvanized by Italia 90 at the same time was purely coincidental.

However, it's not simply changes to football that have contributed to growing female attendances. The changing nature of gender roles between men and women has also had its part to play, being described by Helen Wilkinson, the Research Director

**3**

at Demos, the independent think-tank, as a 'genderquake'. There's a fundamental role reversal going on, gathering pace through the generations. In previous male working-class heartlands like South Wales, there are more women working than men. At schools, colleges and universities, the educational achievements of girls and women are outstripping their male counterparts. From new lasses to Tank Girl, via the female sex-satiated mags like *Sugar*, *More* and *Minx*, women are taking the lads of *Loaded* on at their own game, and coming up winners. It is the height of gender irony that the pretty young things at Manchester United and Liverpool – Beckham, Giggs, McAteer and Redknapp – are skittishly patronized as the 'Spice Boys'. No football fan herself, Helen Wilkinson can nevertheless relate to all this: 'Gender roles are converging, women are becoming more masculine, attached to risk, hedonism and living on the edge, while men are becoming more feminine.'

Female attendance has also been fuelled by the blossoming of a vibrant football culture beyond the boundaries of the local ground. Over the past seven years there has been an explosion of football-related magazines. Whereas once these spoke only to a kids' audience, now they are predominantly for adults. Then there's the proliferation of TV programmes – including two Sky Sports channels – that devote a good measure of their airspace to the game. And Radio 5 Live has built up a fast-growing listener-base where once there was virtually nothing, by providing round-the-clock sports news and live football commentary most nights of the week, plus, of course, a showpiece match every Saturday and Sunday afternoon. Football is big, very big news: from the publishing phenomenon that was *Fever*

*Pitch* (now taking its place on the silver screen too); the elevation of the football kit to the rank of fashion accessory; *Fantasy Football* – the game and the TV show; to the ranks of politicians, comedians and musicians who spill forth a constant stream of terrace tales. The national newspapers show this growth more than anything else: once football was tucked away in the back pages, today it has spread on to the feature, the news, and even the financial pages, and brings in its wake complete pull-out sports sections and give-away magazines stuffed full of match reports. With this kind of profile, it's hardly a big surprise that a fair number of women are starting to elbow their way into football, out of curiosity if nothing else.

With the football media multiplying at a furious rate, the spaces for women journalists, presenters and photographers have increased too. Astute editors and producers are realizing that the same old diet of ex-pros treating us to the most hackneyed phrases imaginable won't satisfy the spaces and audiences these new media are creating. As women football journalists and presenters grow in prominence, they are fuelling other womens' willingness to think of football as their own. As any good philosopher knows, it's a dialectical relationship, and for us women it's beginning to work to our benefit. It's a relationship that gives other women the confidence to assert their right to be at football. As Radio 5 Live presenter Eleanor Oldroyd puts it: 'If a woman is in a pub and her boyfriend is talking over her, and refuses to let her make her point, she can challenge him: 'How can you say women don't know anything about football when Radio 5 employs women to present their football shows?'

Of course it is wrong to think that women going to football is something completely new. In the late twentieth century there is rarely, if ever, anything that's really new, just different. So we learn that in fact women have been following, and playing, the game for at least as long as the men. Most of us never learn this precious fact about our forebears because football's history is constructed in such a way that it makes these women pioneers absent, almost invisible. Football glories in its precious past: from the 20s and 30s of players with shorts down to their knees and the Wembley policeman on his white horse, to the long-haired maverick of the 70s rushing, panting, down the wing after a late night out with his glamorous girlfriend, or that gentleman of the turf, Bobby Moore, being lifted on to the shoulders of his team-mates with the gleaming Jule...

women fit into these p...

wives, daughters and mot...

who stood on those heaving m...

old? Who kept the spirit of women ...

days of the FA ban? Writing women foo...

enables the men of today to treat us as john...

more accurately joanna-come-latelies, when in ...

have been there all along.

In the past, women fans have been prevented from following
football week in week out because of family responsibilities –
childcare and domestic chores have always fallen more heavily on
them. And who knows how many women were prevented from
ever going to a game: by husbands who believed football was for
men only, or the fact that the very culture of football seemed so
closed and forbidding. Women in the past – and in the main even
now – have needed someone, usually a man, to introduce them to
the game: to take them inside those exclusive walls. Often such
invitations weren't forthcoming. As Chelsea fan Debbie Tor puts
it: 'My dad sat my brother down in front of the TV to watch the
FA Cup final, but gave me and my sister lollipops and told us to
go and play quietly upstairs. I felt so rejected. Why wasn't I
important enough to be asked? My dad just assumed that football was for boys.'

female attendances have ebbed
through history according to levels of violent
behaviour. When the game had a reputation for roughness and
hooliganism, women stayed away. Maisie Morrish is a case in
point: 'I stopped going to away games during the 1970s when
we had stones hurled at us after a game against Stoke City. My
husband and I were crouched in a doorway as these yobs threw
bricks, stones, bottles – you name it – at one another. I thought:
"This is just too rough for ladies."' Vice-chair of the Football
Supporters Association Shiela Spiers has always hated the
violence that attaches itself to football but refused to let it stop
her from supporting Liverpool. 'I'd seen lots of fighting outside
grounds in the 70s but it was young lads fighting one another.
I had a saying: "Put a cage up outside the ground, chuck them
in, charge them ten bob and let them fight the hell out of one
another." Because if you went to a game and you didn't want
to get involved in it, you didn't have to. 'That was until she went
to an away game against Tottenham: 'After the game I saw a little
lad who'd been caught in the midst of this swathe of fighting that
had kicked off. I ran up the side street to get him out of the way
but before I reached him someone grabbed hold of him, spun
him round and literally tore the sleeve of his coat off. The poor
lad had a big bruise on the side of his face. When you see kids
involved, it's sickening. I didn't go to another away match in
London until 1990.'

But Shiela does think those dismal days are largely over –
although the continuing presence of small-scale fights most
Saturdays at some game or another shows the potential for

trouble is always there. Better policing, stewarding, heavy penalties, banning orders and closed-circuit television have all had an effect, as has the changing nature of youth culture and indeed masculinity. As Shiela puts it: 'In the 70s and 80s, the culture revolved around being a tough guy, pitting our hard gang against your lot. It goes back to the cult of the great British war hero, you put on a uniform and you have to defend it. That still happens occasionally, but it tends to be amongst older men – in their 30s and 40s – who've grown up doing it and not grown out of it. But young people's culture has changed. It's no longer the done thing to be a hooligan, kids are now into raving and taking drugs that make you feel relaxed and happy.' If violence is a factor that prohibits women attending, the prognosis for new female fans maintaining their links with the game looks promising.

But if more women are going to games and the stadia facilities are better and more welcoming, we shouldn't run away with the idea that a brave new dawn is upon us, not just yet. Women still only have a delicate toe-hold in this heavily male culture. They still have to fight to be taken seriously as fans. As comedian Jo Brand rightly recognizes, patronizing attitudes are never far away: 'Men

9

jealously guard the game. They developed the concept of the real football fan – male – and the slightly crap one – female.' We have a situation where swathes of new female fans are desperately trying to connect with football's hallowed traditions from a position of relative weakness. After all, football is intrinsic to masculinity. Many men grow up playing football, swapping Panini stickers in the play ground, reading *Rothman's Year Books* and developing some knowledge of the game even if they don't go week in week out. Women tend not to have that life-long, multi-faceted, relationship with the game, although as it becomes more acceptable for women to go to football – less of a risk to their femininity – this may well change. For the women fans new to football, this male obsession with history – an essential part of football's culture – is daunting. Female fans do endeavour to 'cram all that information in our heads', as one fan put it to me, in a spirit of trying to gain acceptance. They want to fit in, not muddy the waters. But until traditional supporters recognize that fans come to the game with different degrees of knowledge and different identifications, women in particular will tend to be at a disadvantage.

Even the old-timers like Shiela Spiers, who knows Liverpool's history inside out, have to put up with being patronized. She describes how a close male friend with whom she regularly attends matches displayed his male wrath at her opinion of the game. '"How would you know?" he said, "you've never played football." And that accusation is one that a man can always make to a woman.' This is why Shiela 'can't think of anything more important' than the fostering of opportunities for women to play football. Indeed, there remains a vital connection between women playing and supporting football.

*One of the Lads* is a book about the women who follow football, who work in it and write about it, providing the informal infrastructures that enable men to manage, play and support. That's not to decry the contribution of women footballers, their story more than deserves a book in itself, it's just this isn't it. If you are interested, have a look on the shelf where you picked this one up and you might find Pete Davies' *I Lost My Heart to the Belles*, Gail Newsham's *In a League of Their Own!*, Sue Lopez' *Women on the Ball*, and David Williamson's *Belles of the Ball*. I will just ask you to bear in mind the point Shiela so forcefully made to me on the day I met her outside Anfield: 'If more women were playing the game it would give them credibility, it would mean that they could not be patronized in the way I was and break down the barriers that maintains football as a sport for men.'

That the Football Association has made real efforts to get more young girls playing is to its credit. Mark Sudbury, the FA's spokesman on women's football, says: 'We want to establish leagues amongst schoolgirls so that they can start playing from an early age. And by setting up the infrastructure, professionalizing the way women's football is run, we hope to attract the best girl athletes to our sport.' Only then will the English game begin to match the strength and depth of teams in the USA and Scandinavia.

Football is also a way in which women can enjoy the same sense of solidarity that many men typically feel when they embark on their Sunday morning ritual of playing a game in the park with the lads. Women who play can enjoy that same sense of togetherness, a tightly-knit clannishness to see you through the highs and lows of a Sunday league season. For Phoenix LFC, there's a further dimension to this bonding, for this is one of the all-lesbian football teams. As Kate Greenwood, club founder and manager bravely puts it: 'Football is a way for us to express our sexuality in a conventional way. We can enjoy being together as lesbian women without having to hide our sexuality like we do in so many other areas of our life.' To use football as a means of asserting their rightful place in everyday society, to put down the bigots who would deny these women the right to be mothers, to marry their partners, even in some cases to employment, is the height of irony. Though unfortunately there remain a fair few who still don't get it and Phoenix have suffered more than their fair share of barracking and physical abuse.

One controversy that the growth in women fans has brought with it concerns our so-called 'civilizing influence'. It is here that the real objections some men have towards women become apparent – usually in an implicit rather than explicit way. Women are resented as the ones responsible for softening the rough edges of the sport. The feeling amongst some men – and indeed women – is that football has transformed itself for the middle class fans. There is talk of a well-heeled takeover, of ordinary working class fans being priced out of the game, in order to accommodate a more wealthy and choosier elite with no intrinsic loyalty to the club, drawn to the all-seater stadia and better catering facilities. Often, new women fans are considered to be part of this middle class takeover. The fact that we are accused of not having followed the team 'man and boy' really does say it all, unfortunately. Our alleged class is being used as a convenient mask to attack our gender.

Yet women and men alike who go to football are teachers, civil servants, shop assistants and nurses. Our working conditions are certainly different to the boilermakers, dockers and miners that once filled the stadia, decades of deindustrialization have killed off the communities that would previously have been defined as football's natural fan base. That's life, and football is simply reflecting that. So when the spirit of class resentment is summoned up from within the male psyche, men are revealing their own sense of loss and transferring their resentment on to us, blaming the presence of women for the eclipse of an identity that will never be reborn.

With our femininity, it is alleged, comes a supposed dilution of the intensity of fandom. Undoubtedly there are cases where male fans do curb their behaviour around female fans, and if that means less racist chanting, fewer extreme obscenities in front of young kids, less casual descent into brutish violence, and fewer thoughtless people blocking everybody's view, then on occasion

13

that's no bad thing. But that is not why women go. And there is no consensus amongst women fans about what constitutes 'civilized' behaviour. Women fans are not some homogeneous bloc with a fully worked out set of moral standards: one woman's idea of civilized behaviour might be another's idea of censorship. It shouldn't be forgotten that plenty of women can swear, drink, stand and sing with the worst of them.

In the same way, there is no single unifying reason why women choose to go to football. Women have as many different connections and identifications with the game as there are female fans. These attachments may be more wide ranging than men's, given that women often come to their club via non-traditional routes. Lyn Jamieson, a vicar from Tyneside and a Newcastle United fan who wears a 1950s replica Newcastle shirt with her clerical collar, found it was the spiritual dimension that drew her to United's St James Park stadium. 'People who sit next to each other but who don't know each other well hug one another at the end of the season. Football brings people together in a very special way, it's a very unique bond. That is very spiritual. I love it.' Sally Hibbin, a film producer and Spurs fan, sees football as her last remaining link with the community she came from, and for Liz Loxley, a poet and Bristol Rovers supporter, 'Football is an opportunity to experience intense emotions in a safe environment. I've been at games where I've shaken so much, felt so sad, that it was unbearable. But the great thing is you know you'll come through it, those feelings do pass. And that knowledge gives me a handle – a wisdom – to cope with the ups and downs of my own life.'

Male fans who believe women can't possibly be good for the game, that we are inherently going to make it softer and less of a macho sport, would do well to take note of the views of the Labour MP and Arsenal fan Kate Hoey. Far from wanting football to become a sanitized entertainment-led spectacle akin to a day out at Alton Towers, she's a passionate champion of the right of fans to stand at football games. She is an equally committed advocate of the right of fans to have a stake in the game they love and support, as befits a fully signed-up Labour modernizer.

But women fans don't have to be in the privileged position of a public figure like Kate Hoey to affect change at football. Our very presence in the stands, or perched up high in a commentary position, drawing up the contracts for the manager's glamorous foreign signings, or playing out on the pitch is more than enough testament to the way we want football's wind blowing. And in the girl power days of the spiced up late 1990s, what better way to remind those lads who like to think we're only there to make up the numbers than Spice Girl Mel C's immortal chat up line: 'I'd give a shy glance then flex my biceps. I'd chat him up with "I've got two tickets for the Liverpool match, do you fancy coming?"' One of the lads? That will do nicely thank you very much.

# Generation Games

## The Women Football Forgot

> For an hour and a half... not only had you escaped from the
> clanking machinery of the lesser life, from work, wages, rent,
> dole, sickpay insurance cards, nagging wives, ailing children,
> bad bosses, idle workmen, but you escaped with most of
> your mates, and your neighbours and half the town, and
> there you were, cheering together, thumping each other on
> the shoulders, swopping judgements like lords of the earth,
> having punched your way through a turnstile and into
> another and altogether more splendid kind of life.
>
> J. B. Priestley, *The Good Companions*

It is tempting to imagine that women never went to football in
J. B. Priestley's day. Football was for him an all male world, an
escape from ailing kids and nagging wives. A world where women
knew their place: while their husbands were letting off steam they
were at home, washing the dishes for Saturday evening supper,
tidying the house, bawling out the kids.

Priestley's is not the only image from the past that excludes women.
Our popular memory of football's past revolves around the great

players: Bobby Moore sitting on the shoulders of Geoff Hurst and Martin Peters after England won the 1966 World cup; the great managers – Shankly, Stein, Busby, Paisley. When we do think of fans, we think of the dirty-faced kids knocking a ball around in some northern backstreet, cloth-capped men trudging to the game straight from a hard morning's work at the factory, and sepia photos of a seemingly all male football crowd. What we don't see are images of women.

But women are there, right at the centre of football's history. Only in a history written by men, for men, the contribution of these women has gone more or less unnoticed. So a whole host of questions are not even raised, let alone answered. Who looked after the kids while those great managers and players were busy making football history? Of those boys who played football, didn't their sisters play too? And who patched up their knees when they fell on those hard stone cobbles? Why have so few people heard of the pioneering women's football team the Dick Kerr's Ladies, who attracted crowds in excess of 50,000? And when those avid male fans went to see their team in a thrilling FA Cup final, who packed their sandwiches?

When it comes to constructing this almighty historical artifice, football, as our national, people's, some even say beautiful, game, women are lost in the mists of time. But they were present. A new breed of radical social historians, borne on a wave of uncovering the realities of life on the terraces, has done much to uncover the hidden history of these women. Rogan Taylor's work is founded on giving a voice, through oral accounts, to the fans of yesteryear.

**18**

He reveals that as early as 1885, Preston North End had to abandon its 'ladies free' concession when some 2,000 female fans turned up. So much for women fans never existing pre-Italia 90, 'Nessun Dorma', and Nick Hornby. John Williams and Jackie Woodhouse of Leicester University's Sir Norman Chester Centre for Football Research suggest in a chapter 'Women and Football in Britain' in *British Football and Sociological Change*, that this Preston explosion of women support was no one-off. In 1929 they record: 'Press reports suggest that "at least 50 per cent" of the trainloads of spectators who were travelling to Wembley to watch Bolton Wanderers and Portsmouth were women.' They go on to say: 'Such were the number of female fans who travelled to Leicester to watch their team, Brentford, in a cup tie in 1936, that the local press dubbed the London club "the ladies team". If, as some claim today, the game has a "family tradition" involving substantial numbers of female fans, the 1920s and early 1930s surely seem as good a reference point as any in its history.' This is not to suggest that football is anything but male-dominated in its past, and present. But as these historical accounts have begun to reveal, there is a distinct women's presence that has a long tradition.

There are reasons why women have and have not gone to football over the course of this century. Some are connected to football's image – women's participation ceases when incidents of violence and disorder increase. Then there is the reality of individual women's lives. While it is impossible to make sweeping judgements about specific women or specific periods in history, the barriers to women's participation as supporters over the years must include: domestic and childcare responsibilities; lack of financial independence

19

– women tended to be brought into the labour force when they were needed and were the first to be let go when they weren't; prejudices of husbands or families; expectations of the women themselves; the fact that until the 1960s social roles were clearly segregated. With reference to the latter, football was deemed to be a masculine activity – indeed it still is. John Williams and Jackie Woodhouse use the work of historian Richard Holt to explain football's long-held associations with masculinity thus: 'Organized football clubs provided the bridge between the world of the child and the adult male world, a world in which boys learned to drink and tell jokes as well as the language of physical aggression. Sport was part of this process. Football clubs were only part of the wider process of male socialization which took place in the workplace, the pub and the world of hobbies... Pubs were places where men both played games and talked about them.' They add that it must have been difficult for women in the past to permeate those masculine enclaves. But there are women who did just that. This is their story.

## It's a family affair

How did women in the past come to go to football? Football is essentially a social activity passed down through families. So the most obvious explanation is that a family member – most likely a father, husband, brother or uncle – took them. Margaret Briggs is a case in point. She has been supporting Preston North End since 1915. Small and slight, with skin as soft and white as powder, Margaret describes how her footballing life began. 'I started going on the terraces with my dad when I was nine. With me being a little girl and the next-to-youngest, he had time to bother with me. It was a treat for me, money was scarce in those days but it was free for girls. I liked the fact that I could spend time with my dad and it was company for him.'

'My dad was a wonderful man,' Margaret says, explaining how she came to be on those Deepdale terraces when none of her other girlfriends were. 'I never expected to go, and he didn't have to take me. Most fathers wouldn't have done – they saw it as a man's pleasure.' It was down to her mother, too. Margaret's three elder brothers were already grown-up by the time Margaret was nine, and with only one young child to look after, her mother didn't need her daughter to help around the house. It was unusual for a women to go to games: 'When I first started going you could spot a few other women – many were much older than me – in their 40s and 50s. We didn't wear trousers and football shirts like they do today, we wore our ordinary clothes, a skirt and jumper. Some of the women wore a scarf in club colours that they'd knitted themselves.'

If football was not a sport they enjoyed as a family – 'I had three brothers but they all went with their friends and my mother wasn't interested at all' – that is not to say the family didn't spend time talking about it. 'My mother used to say: "They'll think we're falling out next door," because each of us had a favourite player and thought that someone else was terrible.' In the midst of this maelstrom was Margaret, the only woman in the family able to share in the conversation. 'My mother sat quietly by. Her view

was: "Let the men talk."' She did have her part to play, though:
she would go and make tea and sandwiches for everyone, just
as she made the hot post-match meal on a Saturday afternoon.

For Pat Kirkham, born in 1945 in the northeastern mining village
of Bedlington, being interested in football seemed perfectly natural.
The culture was steeped in football, so much so that Pat can't talk
about her childhood without it cropping up. 'I can't remember not
having experiences of football,' she says simply. 'It was just assumed
I would be involved, which in a sense is even more powerful.'

Her earliest memory – before she was five – is of going with her
father to cheer on her brother at a junior football game. Her next is
of playing football in the backstreets, 'with varying degrees of balls',
with 'Roy next door' and his male friends. 'He would be running up
and down the street saying "Please let her play," because of course
the other boys thought it was sissy playing with a girl.'

Then there was the whole new world that opened up when her
brother signed professional terms with Burnley in 1956. It became
customary for well-known footballers of the day to come round

to the house: the Charltons who lived in the next village (whose mother Cissie 'was seen as this pushy woman who screamed at her sons from the sidelines'), Newcastle United's Frank Brennan, and the Burnley players Jimmy Mcilroy, Jimmy Adamson and, the object of Pat's first teenage crush, Jimmy Robson. 'I've still got his photo,' she admits, and sure enough, out of the draw of her desk in the university history department where she is now a professor, she takes a picture of a tall, lean young man with a classic 50s crew cut, a dark-haired version of James Dean. Not that Pat needs a picture, she sees Jimmy at family events. Now slightly balding, he still lives in Bedlington where he is the local milkman.

The most significant person in shaping her football experiences was her father. She and her father always went to games together – whether it was to follow her brother's career or her father's club, Newcastle United – until Pat left home to go to university. 'I have strong memories of standing in Newcastle's popular end with my dad's arms around me when we were crushed together. And he never batted an eyelid at the swearing, perhaps he thought it was best to pretend it wasn't happening. Occasionally another fan would point it out: "Hey, curb your fucking language, can't you ee there's a fucking kid here?" They had no idea they were swearing,' she laughs.

Pat felt comfortable in this male environment because her father never suggested it was unusual. But she did notice there were very few other girls. 'Although I was accepted by my father's friends, they never took their kids – male or female. I sometimes went with the father of a girl in my class but she never went. I don't even know if some of the men even had kids.'

Pat's parents were unusual for the time – and the locality – in being very progressive and open-minded. Pat's mother was an early feminist who fought her way into the working men's clubs at a time when they were seen as an all male preserve. Her father, who had himself been offered a scholarship to grammar school – he was unable to take it up after his father forced him to leave school to work in the pits – relished having an eager and intelligent child with whom he could share his interests. 'He always treated me like an adult,' Pat explains. 'He assumed I knew incredible details: who Huddersfield's reserve goalkeeper was, the footballing history of quite minor local players. He never got angry if I couldn't remember, he would try and encourage me – "Oh Pat, you know that" – and amazingly, most of the time I did.'

But again, it wasn't a family game as such. Pat's mother did not like football. She saw only the dangerous and aggressive side – as many mothers did – and worried constantly that her son was going to be injured. Indeed, having seen him knocked unconscious and losing half a mouthful of teeth, it is hardly surprising she was so negative. 'My brother collided with a goalkeeper in a junior football game and of course my mother and I were frantic,' Pat explains. 'Minutes later the opposing fans shouted to the goalkeeper: "You should have killed the bastard!" My mother was disgusted: "That's my son, you're talking about."' She was so angry that Pat's father had to restrain her; she was going to give them a piece of her mind. 'My dad had to explain that this was football, that they didn't want to listen to her.'

While Pat's mother found football unpalatable, she didn't let that stand in the way of her daughter going; she felt it was up to Pat to make up her own mind. 'It was probably a great boon for her to get me off her hands for an afternoon,' Pat says. She certainly never gave Pat any indication that going to football was an 'unfeminine' activity for a girl. Rather her tone was one of bemused silence at the exploits of her daughter. If she couldn't share her excitement, she certainly didn't mock it. 'I can remember coming home from football the day the offside rule clicked,' Pat says. 'I was seven and it was a real rite of passage for me. My dad would explain it, but there's nothing like that magical moment when you scream "offside" at the moment the player kicks the ball. My father was so excited he shouted out to my mother: "Gladys, you'll never guess what she's done!" I don't know what she thought when he blurted out: "She knows her offsides!"'

For Pat, football is an integral part of her identity. Despite the fact that she no longer lives in Bedlington, it connects her with her roots, with the working class culture in which she grew up – so much so, that when she went to university she felt embarrassed about going to football with the middle class students she met there. Rather then seeing football in terms of gendered differences, Pat saw class divides. 'There was this sense of watching someone observing your class. It was problematic for me. I'd think: "Why do you want to be here?"'

It isn't the case that Pat became a fan simply because of her class, because of the culture in which she grew up. She didn't simply imbibe football as if by osmosis – after all, most of her girlfriends

25

did not go. Pat went because her father encouraged her involvement in a positive way. He did not take her because he didn't have a son to take, but because he wanted her to get the same enjoyment out of football that he did. He protected her when he thought it necessary, but was not overbearing. And he was never patronizing. He did not say: 'You're very knowledgeable about football for a girl,' as some fathers are wont to do.

## The people's game is not for everyone

Many women – past and present – do not have the harmonious associations that Pat Kirkham has. They have put up with sexism and prejudice. Shiela Spiers, who started supporting Liverpool as an 11-year-old in 1948, recalls the looks of incredulity on the faces of the men who frequented her father's pub when word got out that he was taking her – a girl – to the 1950 FA Cup final at Wembley. 'Their attitude was very strange: how can this girl be going to a cup final? In those days, Liverpool's gates were over 50,000 and Liverpool got 15,000 FA Cup tickets, so only a small number of supporters could go. There was a certain amount of envy of anyone who had a ticket, but particularly for a girl, it was considered a complete waste. But the men I knew well said: "Show us your ticket." Some of them had never seen one before.'

Shiela puts their attitude down to the way society was organized in postwar Britain. 'Football reflects society. In the 1940s there were preserves for men and preserves for women. It was unusual for a couple to go out together on a regular basis. If a man wanted to go out in the evening, he went to the pub with his mates. If he followed football he wouldn't think to take his wife. You just accepted that men and women had different roles. But society wouldn't accept that today.'

It might be expected that attitudes would have changed by the late 60s, but not where the traditions of football were concerned. Shiela's brother was outraged when he found out she intended to go on Liverpool's hallowed Kop. 'Women on the Kop, never,' she raises her eyebrows in mock horror. 'My brother stood outside the ground with me until I managed to swap my ticket for one in another part of the stadium. And I just accepted that.'

While her brother phrased his objections in terms of concern for her safety – she might get crushed in the crowd, she wouldn't be able to see – his real motive was to preserve the honour of the Kop, to keep it all male. 'It was sexist,' she says. 'If you look at footage of the Kop singing Beatles songs in the 60s, you can see it was all male. The young men were in the centre where they could be boisterous and loud, and the older people stood further back or at the sides where they would be more comfortable.' It was only in the late 70s and 80s that women started to go on Liverpool's Kop, and then not without hostile reactions. As Shiela explains: 'The first women that went in were regarded as tarts. I've been coming out of the ground and I've heard fellas say: "She's only in here because she wants to get felt up." It was a territorial response, men saw the Kop as the place they went to get away from women.'

Jean Thomasson may not have encountered such overt pressure but she has felt the full weight of society's disapproval. Jean followed Bolton as a schoolgirl in the late 40s, going first with her father and then with her best friend Margaret. 'It was an alternative to following a pop star,' Jean explains, 'because after the Second World War there just weren't any music stars, and footballers, you could see them every week. Admission to the ground then,' Jean laughs, 'was only four pence.'

Jean and Margaret had typical schoolgirl crushes on their favourite players – Jean's was on the goalkeeper Stan Hanson, Margaret's on the now legendary centre forward Nat Lofthouse. 'We used to pester them to death,' she recalls. 'We'd go round to their houses carol singing in November, take fireworks down on bonfire night, we even found out what bus they took to training – we just wanted to see them.'

Jean, aged 13, even wrote a poem for Stan:

> Saw a man in a green polo
> Down at Burnden Park
> Now he lives in Springfield Road

28

Grand place in the dark.
Do I love him? Do I love him?
'Yes, on your life.'
Can I have him? Can I have him?
'No, he has a wife.'
Living down on Harper Green,
Not far from his home
At the end of every day,
Round his place I roam.
Who makes my heart sing
'Yippi Yi, Yippi Yo'?
The goalie in the green polo.

For Jean, going to football appears to be an early sign of an independent character. She was aware that very few of her girlfriends were fans – she never talked about football at school – but resolved to go anyway. 'I was quite outspoken as a girl and determined to do what I wanted.' But as adulthood beckoned, it became less acceptable for the two young women to follow Bolton.

It's a familiar story amongst women of Jean's generation. Going to football, like being a tomboy, was considered a harmless phase that some girls went through, but they were expected to grow out of it. They were expected to settle down, get married and start a family, to dedicate themselves to their husband and children at the expense of their own interests. As Queens Park Rangers fan Caroline Coon puts it: 'It's a tragedy of what happens to women once they escape teenagehood and are expected to become responsible and caring.

29

The pop concert, the football arena are places where girls can be hysterical and wet their knickers with sexual glee, have their male heroes. But society trivializes these emotions, lest you forget that once you reach 16 you have to become a mature and sensible woman.'

As Jean realized when she became an adult, there were other assumptions cast on her reasons for following Bolton. 'In the 1950s there were clear rules about what was acceptable behaviour for men and women. The view was that the women who went to football were either after a man and weren't too fussed how they got one, or were so unfeminine as to be drawn to masculine activities.' This societal pressure proved too much for Margaret: she stopped being a supporter once they left school at 16. 'To be quite honest,' Jean says, 'I think she's ashamed of going, she doesn't want anyone to know. People have a mental image of a football fan and that doesn't represent her now.'

Jean did carry on supporting Bolton right through her university years, but just as convention stipulated, once she got married in 1959 her participation died away. Her husband, an armchair-supporting Manchester United fan, did not approve. 'I was very much the wife at home, I didn't have a say in anything really. I did go to games a couple of times when we first married but my husband didn't like it, he would get upset if I was out too long. Women just didn't have the independence that they do today,' she says. The only other live games Jean did see in the early years of her marriage were at Old Trafford. 'We moved out of Bolton, so I lost touch with my club or I don't think I could have done it,' she admits.

**30**

Jean may have been a far more ardent fan than her husband but he was not about to change his own lukewarm allegiance to suit her. Neither was he willing to compromise: to go to both Bolton and Manchester United games. But as Jean says: 'I had to like it or lump it. I don't drive, so it's not as if I could just jump in the car and go off and do my own thing. I was very dependent on him in that sense.'

Margaret Briggs was also dependent on her husband. 'I was lucky,' she says. 'My husband looked after me. Whenever he went to the game he always bought me a ticket, too.' It may not have been so easy for Margaret had her husband decided he wanted to go to Preston North End with his male friends. Margaret stopped working once she married in 1930, so asserting her independence – going out and buying her own ticket – may well have been difficult when her husband ultimately held the purse strings.

Though women fans haven't always had the independence that their husbands and boyfriends enjoyed, this has not affected the ties they have to their teams. Women are, the surveys tell us – more loyal to their clubs, more likely, for example, to buy a season ticket. But aren't the men the ones with the commitment and women the 'fair-weather' supporters? Look behind the image and a different story begins to appear. Christine Geraghty, a Queens Park Rangers supporter and lecturer in media studies at Goldsmiths' College, London, offers this analysis: 'It would be wrong to think football is all about fans who religiously follow one club. There have always been floating supporters. And men are more free to do that floating around.' Christine suggests that men, particularly in the past, have found it easier to be geographically mobile and were far more likely

31

to go to games on their own. Women, on the other hand, 'once they know how to get into the ground – football clubs can seem very closed to outsiders – are more like to carry on going to the place that they know. It's that sense of security, about knowing where it's safe to stand and sit and where the best view is.'

For many women in the past, and indeed today, having children makes increasing demands on their time. Women are still by and large primarily responsible for taking care of the children, often at the expense of their own interests. As Jean Thomasson says: 'As a woman you tend to think that your kids should be your first priority, that you should stay at home with them. That burden still falls to us.'

It's a point Chris Hodson, a Manchester United fan living in Swindon, agrees with. She took time out in the mid 1960s when she had her children. 'It's only in the last ten years, since the kids have reached their teens, that I've started going to every home game again. My husband, not a fan himself, never had any problem with my going but I always felt worried about leaving the kids for long periods. It's acceptable for a wife to stay at home and look after the kids while her husband goes to football but doing it the other way round is not so easy. You feel like you're going to be branded a bad mother for going off and enjoying yourself.' Even today it is easy to see why Chris felt like that: single mothers, working mothers, absent mothers – are they not at the centre of the moral crisis over the family? Aren't mothers still held responsible for everything from unruly kids to falling educational standards? Chris also worked full time, so finding time for her own interests was difficult; weekends tended to be overtaken with household chores.

Some women do manage to combine football and motherhood. Margaret Briggs was one such woman. Crucially, she had the support of her husband. Going to football was an interest they shared together: 'It was an important part of our marriage,' she says. 'I think it's important for a wife to take an interest in her husband's pleasure.' So when Margaret found she was expecting – 'I was in my late 30s and we'd given up on having children' – they worked round fitting football into their family life. 'We'd got so used to following Preston home and away, just getting in the car and driving off for the day, that once my son was born we were too set in our ways to stop. If he'd been born earlier we might not have done that.'

## Independence days

Many women do reassert their independence and return to football once their mothering duties have subsided. But it's not always easy. A man would probably have few qualms about going to games on his own, but for a woman, says Chris Hodson, it can be a daunting prospect. 'Situations change over time, the people you once went with may not be around anymore. So you might find yourself with no one to go with – I did. And I was afraid to go on my own. Not in the sense of being thumped but because it was a very inappropriate thing for a woman to do. It doesn't sound very brave but I'd been brought up to believe you didn't even go to the pictures on your own, never mind football. I had to fight against all that conditioning and say to myself: "If you really want to do it, then go." And that's what I did.'

33

Gina Gatland might not have returned to Spurs but for a chance meeting with Angela, the friend she had gone to games with back in the 1960s. 'Fate brought us together,' she says, recounting the tale of how they met 20 years later on a number 16 bus at Victoria. 'It was as if neither of us had aged, we remembered each other as we had been before we married, and we thought: "Why not?" Let's go back to Spurs.' Angela takes up the story – a common occurrence with these two close friends who, with their blonde hair and round jolly faces, not only look alike but think alike, finishing each other's sentences. 'When you get engaged your life changes. You have different priorities so we lost touch completely. Neither of us went, you can't really afford it when you're bringing up a family and only working part time. But when we met again, it was at a time in our lives where financially and timewise we could say: "We'll do our own thing."'

Not that it hasn't caused ructions in their families. 'My husband has found it difficult,' Gina explains. 'It was alright to begin with, when it was just every home game. When we started going away and I'd be coming home at all hours in the night, it pushed the whole household into disruption, or so he thought. He doesn't now. I say: "You've got a choice of that, that, or that in the fridge, have what you want." But he's dreading the day Spurs get into Europe. He doesn't like the idea that I might be away for more than a day.'

Angela and Gina are living proof that life begins at 40. They have taken an opportunity to relive their youth, to carry on where they left off before marriage and kids intervened. With their crushes on

Spurs players – 'I idolized that man,' Gina says of Jurgen Klinsmann with a sigh any 16-year-old Boyzone fan could relate to – it's as though they too are 16 again. 'Sometimes I can't believe what I'm doing,' she says, describing how she converted one of her best lemon sheets into a banner, with the words 'Jurgen please stay' written in blue paint – 'that cost £6 and took two days to dry on the line' – in a vain attempt to keep the German international at Spurs. 'I thrust it up as high as I could when we got to the match so he could see it.' She and Angela burst into giggles. 'Can you believe it,' Gina adds, 'I'm 56 years old and I'm acting like a little groupie.

Changes in society have made it easier for women like Gina and Angela – of the post-war baby boom generation – to assert their independence and return to football, or in some cases carry on going to football taking the kids with them. Since the 1960s more women have entered the workforce and earn their own living; labour-saving devices like the washing machine, microwave and dishwasher help make light work of household chores; the contraceptive pill gives women and men greater control over planning their families; the greater flexibility brought by late-night shopping allows us to manage our leisure time better; and social roles between men and women have gradually begun to break down, with couples spending more time together in family pursuits.

Sue Wallis, 50, a Manchester City fan and mother of three says she has seen changes in her own life over the last 30 years: 'More women do have time on their hands. I don't go shopping on a Saturday afternoon anymore, I go with my husband in the evening.

And I think there are other women just like me. So when our
husbands say: "I'm going to the match," we're likely to say: "I'll
come with you."'

Sue believes that more women are demanding a right to a
'playtime' just like their husbands and boyfriends. 'Women of my
generation never questioned the right of men to go off and enjoy
themselves, and we never demanded the same for ourselves. But
today we are working just as hard as men – well we always have,
but housework isn't always recognized as real work is it? In the
past our part-time jobs didn't have the same status, it was the men
who brought home the family wage. Now though, we're doing
the same jobs as the men and we want to play just as hard.'

Of course the opportunities for individual women to take
advantages of these societal changes vary widely. As Chris Hodson
says: 'I'd like to think it's easier for women today – it's become far
more acceptable for women to work and have a family and to have
their own independence. But when I go on the away coach, it's all
men. So we shouldn't get carried away, women are still in the
minority. And there are still men who want to keep it that way.'

Neither should we imagine that women in the past did not assert
their right to go to games despite the difficulties they had looking
after the family, doing hours of unpaid housework, and often
holding down low-paid jobs.

# Knickerbocker glories

Women in the past haven't just watched football, they have played, too. David Williamson is one of a tiny band of sports historians who have charted the origins of women's football. In his excellent book *Belles of the Ball*, he says that as early as 1895, Nettie Honeyball, secretary of the British ladies team, played in a pioneering match between the North and South of England. Performing in front of a packed ground in London's Crouch End, the North won 7–1, but the *Manchester Guardian*'s report concentrated less on the game and more on the 'rational dress': the 'red blouses and white yolks, and full black knickerbockers fastened below the knee'. But such games were undoubtedly few and far between – Victorian society considered football an unsuitable sport for women on account of its roughness – and when women's matches did take place they were at best considered a novelty that would never attract the crowds.

John Williams and Jackie Woodhouse have also chronicled this hidden history in 'Women and Football in Britain'. They found that the First World War aided the development of the women's game. For the first time, whole swathes of women – the hidden labour force – were required to work in the munitions factories and on the land in occupations that had formerly been the preserve of men. This, coupled with the ongoing struggle for political emancipation, created the catalyst for the incredible growth in the popularity of women's football. As David Williamson puts it: 'The women workers desperately needed to have some form of distraction from the war, the work, and the hardship they both brought… the new-found spirit of change and the sense of camaraderie was the perfect

37

recipe for a team game that could help them to let off steam.' Other factors were also crucial to the success of these local factory teams which grew up particularly in the North, the Midlands and the Southwest. Firstly, the fact that the women played for charity was crucial in gaining them the support of the FA and the use of its pitches. Secondly, the men's game was suspended as a result of the war and this meant women were not seen as trying to steal the crowds away from the men's game. Thirdly, the women often played in novelty costumes and this suggested they were not taking their football too seriously.

The most famous of the women's teams was the Dick Kerr's Ladies, formed by a group of munitions workers at the Kerr's engineering factory in Preston in 1917. They may have started out playing on the waste ground outside the factory gates but by 1920 they were attracting massive crowds: 53,000 supporters – with a further 10–14,000 locked out of the ground – came to watch them play against St Helens. They were serious about their football: in that same year, of the 30 games they played, they lost but five. They went on to become the unofficial England team playing internationals against Scotland and France.

Williamson describes the success of women's football thus: 'By early 1921, it was as if the country had been gripped by ladies' football fever. Teams now covered the country, with every major town having its own side and the major cities having several, especially in the North. Whether at the weekend or in the middle of the week, there was a ladies' match being played somewhere.'

But it was not to last. As John Williams and Jackie Woodhouse explain: 'A number of things conspired in the game's sudden downfall. For one thing, the charitable causes and the social context of wartime Britain upon which the game was built… were by 1921 beginning to fade from collective memory. For another, and more importantly, the relative success of the female game and the very seriousness with which some female players and their supporters were now approaching the sport, grated with those powerful opponents who continued to preach about the "defeminizing" dangers of female athleticism. Finally, and most importantly of all, the women's game offended the middle class propriety of the FA's ruling council and, more particularly, it threatened to continue to grab some of the local limelight from the lower ranks of the male game.' After an unsubstantiated corruption charge, the FA was able to distance itself from the women's game. In December 1921 it stated that 'the game of football is quite unsuitable for females and should not be encouraged'. Women's games could no longer be staged on FA pitches. It was a decision that was not revoked until 1971.

Without this meddling, the 'people's game' might have developed in a different way: played by men and women alike, separately, but on an equal basis. As Gail Newsham, author of a history of Dick Kerr's Ladies, *In a League of Their Own!* told me: 'Whole generations of women have grown up thinking women's football is banned, therefore it must be "unnatural". We've got to go about changing it back, and that will take a long time.'

Despite the FA's attitude in the 1920s it would be wrong to assume that generations of budding women footballers simply abandoned

39

playing. Men may have tried to keep women out of 'their game' but women refused to be excluded. Take 75-year-old Joan Whalley. Joan played her first game for the legendary Dick Kerr's Ladies who were still going strong, despite the ban, in 1937. Her career spanned 22 years and she prides herself on 'never missing a game'. She worked as a nurse, a bus conductress – jobs where she could work shifts – so that she could fit in her first love, football. Who knows, if Joan had been born a man she may well be a household name today, just like her childhood pal, the magnificent Preston North End and England winger, Tom Finney. Yet today little is known of Joan's footballing achievements. She is part of football's hidden history. Not that she is complaining. 'Football was my life,' she says. 'I was going to play whatever the odds stacked against me.'

Indeed it seems as if Joan was always destined to play football. At least that's the way her father saw it. He bought Joan her first pair of football boots and a real leather ball for her fifth birthday. It made her very popular with the local lads: 'They always used to come and call for me,' she says, 'because I was the only one with a ball.' And Joan liked nothing better. 'Everyone knew me on the park, my blonde hair would be flying out in the wind as I was racing along with the boys.' They were happy days. Innocent days, when none of society's expectations were apparent. That was to come later. It was only when adolescence beckoned that Joan realized the odds were stacked against her realizing her dream.

## There are two teams in Preston

'Tom Finney and I used to play football all the time,' she recalls.
After the game they would talk about their hopes for the future.
'He always used to say his ambition was to play for a men's football
team. I said mine was to play for a ladies' team if only I could find
one.' They may have been two gifted players, two creative mid-
fielders – they both played on the right wing – but as childhood
merged into adulthood the opportunities open to them could not
have been more different. 'I always told Tom he was lucky, he could
play for Preston North End. Everyone knew who they were. I'd only
heard snatches about the Dick Kerr's Ladies and I didn't know how
you got to play for them.'

After the FA banned women's football, the game went underground.
Teams like the Dick Kerr's Ladies played in pub car parks, at local
showgrounds, festivals and charity events. But these were not likely
to put them in the public eye. Despite living in Preston, Joan had only
a scant knowledge of Dick Kerr's existence. It was purely by chance
that Joan was to find her team. She happened upon Alfred 'Pop'
Frankland's grocer's shop. 'I didn't walk in those days, I bounced,'
she says, and when the grocer remarked on her fitness she told him
of her ambition to play football. No wonder his ears picked up,
Alfred was the manager of Dick Kerr's Ladies. He offered her a trial.
'I've never run so fast in my life,' she says. 'I wanted to get home to
tell my mother I'd found a manager.' The rest, as they say, is history.

Joan remembers her first game. It took place on 12 May 1937,
Coronation Day, at Roundhay Park in Leeds. 'I'm a very shy person.

41

And sitting in that dressing room I had terrible butterflies. But the other Dick Kerr's players were older than me – I was only 15 – and took me under their wing.' Including the great Lilly Parr, who Gail Newsham describes as 'probably the best footballer of all time': so ferocious was her shot that when a male player laughingly suggested she was no match for him, she blasted the ball into the back of the net with such force that he broke his arm trying to stop it. 'I was at the end of the line as we marched out onto the pitch with the crowd cheering. I was shaking with nerves until that whistle went and then I forgot everything. That's the marvellous thing about football, you enter another world.' She shuffles her feet. 'I just wish I could get back there now.'

The large crowd that gathered to celebrate King George VI's coronation was not a one-off. Gail Newsham estimates that the average crowd in the 30s was around 5,000. 'We used to get a lot of families,' Joan recalls. 'Women would come to see what women's football was like, and the men came to taunt and jeer. "Get 'em off," "Women can't play," they'd shout, but after ten minutes they realized we could play, and then it was: "Come on Blondie, swing it in!" It was marvellous.'

Joan has never married, preferring to commit herself to football. 'If you play sport you have to give your whole self to it, you can't have a husband and kids in the background. Women do still take most of the responsibility for looking after the family. Imagine telling the manager: "I can't play today, my son's got chicken pox"? A man would play even if his son had a temperature of 102, he'd leave his wife to deal with it.' Joan admits most of the Dick Kerr's

Ladies combined their football and a family life, but this was not for her. 'I'm far too independent to have any man telling me what to do. I had a boyfriend when I was 17. And when he suggested we got engaged I told him: "No way, I'm footballing."'

Dick Kerr's didn't always have brilliant venues: 'We played anywhere we could: pub car parks, cinder tracks, farmers' fields where the grass was so long we could barely see the ball.' They may not have received the publicity that Preston North End did, and they may not have made a penny out of playing, but Joan still believes it was easier than the women struggling to finance their clubs have it today. 'We had no money worries: we didn't have to pay out of our own pockets for hotels, referees, pitches or transport. All we had to do was turn up.' It's a point Gail Newsham agrees with: 'The ban on women's football may have lifted, but how much has the FA's attitude changed? We may have a national league now, there may even be a bit of media coverage, but our women's Premier League footballers are broke. They've still got to pay to play, there's no funding for them. Even the England squad still have to take time off work to play abroad, and they don't get compensation – they have to pay to represent their country.'

Joan played her own part in popularizing women's football when she agreed to take part in a Nike advertising campaign in 1995 promoting a new range of women's trainers with sporting heroines of the past fronting the 48 sheet posters and double-page spreads. 'Does this look like me?' Joan demanded of me as she whipped out one of these adverts from the drawer. 'I look like a creature from the black lagoon.' Joan had been mistakenly under the impression

43

that by modelling for the fashion shoot she might be doing her bit, via Nike, to promote women's football to an up-and-coming generation. But not any more: 'Young girls will take one look at me and think: "I'm not taking up football if you end up looking like that,"' she spluttered. Nike's aim was undoubtedly to shift a few more thousand units. Nevertheless, Joan didn't leave me with doom and gloom. However cack-handedly, here was one of the major players in the sportswear economy taking the trouble to revisit our past, to popularize a history that has scarcely been written about apart from by a handful of peculiarly dedicated historians like David Williamson and Gail Newsham.

As for the women fans of yesteryear, it's almost as if they never existed. But they did exist, and in finding out the conditions that determined their hard-fought-for survival on the margins of the game, we understand better why the people's game became a man's game and how it could yet, multinational makeovers notwithstanding, be a sport genuinely for all.

# Femme Fever Pitch

## Why Can't a Woman Be More Like a Fan?

> I fell in love with football as I was later to fall in love with
> women: suddenly, inexplicably, uncritically giving no thought
> to the pain or disruption it would bring with it.

These are the immortal words with which Nick Hornby opens his
best-selling book *Fever Pitch*.

It is his attempt to get some handle on an obsession 'that began
while I was a schoolboy and endured for more than a quarter of a
century, longer than any relationship I have made of my own free
will'. As he goes on to explain, he loves his family but 'they were
rather foisted on me', he has not kept in contact with friends from
school 'apart from the only other Arsenal fan': football is the one
relationship that has survived. Hornby desperately wants to know
why, for he can see it's 'unhealthy', 'pathological', 'more rigid than
any marriage', that it stops him getting on with his life, and for
what? It's not even as if Arsenal makes him blissfully happy week in
week out: it's made him miserable, inspired feelings of sorrow and
of genuine hatred. Yet he sticks with it. Like any passionate affair,
it ultimately inspires real love. For there is always the next game to

look forward to, all those hopes of victory, that sense of belonging, being part of a crowd who all feel the same, of caring deeply about something that will always be there, that will never turn round and say "I don't love you anymore."'

This story of the agony and ecstasy of fandom, quite unexpectedly sparked off a publishing revolution. Football became a subject people wanted to read and write about. The 'soccerati' was born. But Hornby also gave birth to a new genre of male writing. For *Fever Pitch* was not a typical football book replete with match reports, statistics and player profiles – although it has elements of all these – it was a more personal affair. Written in that most feminine and feminist of genres, the confessional, it was as much about masculinity as football. It was about why football is so important to men. It's not just football, there does seem to be something attractive to men about obsessive fandom and hobbies – for as the whole spate of books that followed *Fever Pitch* show, there are plenty more Nick Hornbys. These were thirty something men trying to get a handle on their particular obsession, including John Aizlewood's eulogy to pop music, *Love is the Drug* (which did incidentally contain two contributions by women) to Nicholas Whittaker's *Platform Souls*, about the life of a trainspotter and Marcus Berkmann's cricket-inspired *The Rain Men*.

Five years on from the publication of *Fever Pitch*, football writing has remained resolutely male. One has only to venture into Sports-pages, London's specialist sports bookshop, to see the extent to which this is true. An obsessive's heaven, a male anorak's dream, it contains row upon row of terrace tales written by men, for men, about the peculiarities of football fandom. Where women are mentioned in these books it tends to be in the negative. Women are the nagging wives, the fair weather female fans who can't hack the wind, rain, sleet and snow, the insensitive mothers-to-be who try to drag their unwilling spouses away from a dreary 0–0 draw to the dramas of the delivery room.

## Bad lads and loose lasses

Women are not centre stage as Jim White, Harry Pearson, Tom Watts, Richard Kurt and a bookshelf of others retell their lives through football. But with the odd misogynistic exception the picture isn't quite as bleak as might first appear. Nick Hornby, and most of the writers who followed in his wake, were influenced by that phenomenon dubbed 'the new man', in touch with their feminine side and all-round softies made good. Rough-edged certainly – no woman was going to rob Nick and his pals of their match-day memories – but they were at least aware of their inadequacies and that if women were pushed too far out of their lives for the sake of football, the game they would be left with wouldn't be quite enough to emotionally sustain them.

'New man' reflects fundamental changes in society. The deregulated market, changing patterns of work – heavy industries have dwindled leaving many men unemployed while vast numbers of women have entered the workforce – the cultural changes brought by feminism, the rise in divorce rates: all these factors produce the situation Jonathan Rutherford, an academic and a writer on masculinity, portrays as: 'contributing to the shifting boundaries between what is home and work. Given that masculine identities are founded around that divide they are obviously going to be seriously disrupted by that.' The new man was one response. The 'new lad' was another.

As journalist Jaci Stephen said in *J'Accuse*, her TV programme on the new lad phenomenon: 'The new man was sensitive, communicative, clitorally correct but alas nauseating. Women disliked him, men loathed him.' But he was at least open to renegotiating his relationship with women. His successor, the adolescent, wolf-whistling, lager loutish 'new lad', has no such motives. 'The new messiah of masculinity is an immature bloke who's only line is "Oh, fancy a shag, top totty." For a whole swathe of males under the age of 35 this is the religion to aspire to.'

Football is central to new laddism in a way it wasn't to the quiche-loving, baby-holding new man. For the new lad is a reaction against the new man, who had allowed himself to be emasculated and dominated by women. New lads were seeking to recapture the deep masculine that the successes of feminism had denied them. And what better place to do that than at football, with its associations of toughness and maleness. Hence football references are redolent throughout the now burgeoning new lad culture. Oasis are Manchester City fans, Blur Chelsea fans, *Loaded*, the magazine for men who should know better, is filled with references to foot-ball. Even fashion has returned to the football casual look of the late 70s and early 80s.

*Fever Pitch* emerged at the same time as all this new laddism. While Nick Horby is no new lad, but more of a bloke really, what he nevertheless likes about football on his first visit 'is the overwhelming maleness of it all – cigar and pipe smoke, foul language'. It's that special atmosphere that cements his passionate commitment. With its overt masculine connotations, football is a place where Hornby and thousands of men like him can celebrate their masculinity, communicate their emotions without being barracked as sissies. It's hardly a big surprise then that *Fever Pitch* can be both read as a classic textbook of new laddism while at the same time having this more subtle, and for women more appealing, soft underbelly of new mannism.

It is this dual purpose that makes *Fever Pitch* such a fascinating read for any woman new to football. Hornby is far more self-conscious than your average lad: he admits to having had therapy, he wants to take his girlfriend to games, he realizes that his obsession is not entirely healthy. For journalist Jon Savage, Hornby is ambivalent about lad culture. Savage says in a *Guardian* article that Hornby offers a list of male faults: 'They become repressed, they fail in their relationships with women, their conversation is trivial and boorish, they find themselves unable to express their emotional needs, they cannot relate to their children, and they die lonely and miserable,' only to end with a dismissive: 'But you know, what the hell.'

Hornby's defence is that he wants to reach out to a wide audience and he cannot do that if he veers too far from the straight and narrow. He is certainly not one of those lads who would claim that women, or indeed the old, the disabled, the black, heaven forbid, the dreaded middle class – anyone that threatens to deprive football's young male heartland of its sacred intensity – should be excluded. He does want the 'people's game' to be for everyone.

A response to the crisis of masculinity that is closer to its femme home is the new lass. A whole generation of women are reacting positively to these uncertain times: buoyed by the successes of women's liberation, and doing better than boys in school, in the job market they are taking intense delight in playing men at their own game. Thatcher's children, these women no longer believe the feminist mantra that women in power would civilize society, or that cooperation should replace competition. Instead they know they can be as tough, hard and demanding as any man. As Helen Wilkinson, of the independent think-tank Demos, wrote in the *Independent:* 'Male and female values are converging, and while feminized new man is still a rare breed, masculinized new woman is ever present. Across the board there are signs that young women are seeking risk and excitement and taking greater pleasure in overt displays of sexuality.' We can see this trend played out in the phenomenal success of the Spice Girls and their creed of 'Girl Power'.

Football is central to new lad culture. It is where the new lad can play out his masculinity with the pack; indulge in a touch of make-believe, or occasionally real, violence, as the crowd of heaving male bodies cries out for some poor unsuspecting fullback's blood; and add a touch of sexual frisson to the proceedings with a hearty dose of 'Get Your Tits Out for the Lads'. Misogyny is alive and well masquerading under that old protective blanket, the joke women can't take. John King pleaded the innocence of irony when *The Football Factory* was published in 1996, but there seems precious little sub-text in passages like: 'You're well fucking pissed on ten pints of lager, with a decent jukebox and a bit of fluff knocking about, mostly slappers in miniskirts, black cotton wedged up their arses, just what you want after a few sherberts.'

Football is not yet nearly as central to new lass culture as it is to the new lads, and as any female fan will certainly recount, there is not much sex to be had at any stadium between the hallowed minutes of kick-off and the final whistle. It's in the after-match nightclubs the new lasses come out to play, but at 3 p.m. on a Saturday afternoon they are more likely to be curled up recovering from the night before.

## Getting in on the act

The women who in increasing numbers are choosing football don't appear in the world of *Fever Pitch*, they are not rated as real fans by the lads, and sit awkwardly with the sex-insatiated new lasses. But they are very much part of modern fandom.

This is how one new wave woman fan, Cathy Long, described what it was like when she first ventured forth onto Liverpool's infamous Kop end in the late 80s: 'I loved it on the Kop. To start with you don't know where to stand, you haven't got your own space yet, so you make the mistake of going in all the wrong places – being in exactly that spot where you're carried along uncontrollably by the crowd rather than safely secured behind a crash barrier. Of course there's a great feeling of freedom, it doesn't matter that you've lost the person you're with because the game is so exciting. You're thinking: "God, they're going to score," you're so wrapped up with what's happening out on the pitch that nothing else matters. I found the atmosphere wonderful as a woman I suppose – although I don't like to think of myself as a woman supporter. But people looked after you, they looked after each other. There was a great feeling of togetherness. How often do you get to be so physically close to people, to have complete strangers hugging you? Or to be able to get hold of the person next to you in absolute joy? You can't do that in any other environment. And every inhibition would go. You could just be yourself. Nothing else mattered to me that afternoon.'

But becoming a fan was not easy. Cathy did not come from a football-supporting family, her girlfriends at school didn't go and she wouldn't have dreamed of going with the boys. It was only in her late teens that she first went to Anfield. 'I was always asking around my friends to see if anyone wanted to go to the game.'

As a girl, Cathy was knowledgeable about football: everyone in her class supported either Liverpool or Everton, she always looked out for the football results on a Saturday afternoon, and in hockey lessons the girls picked their positions according to the position of their favourite football players. Not to know about football in Liverpool in the 1970s was to ignore an enormous part of the local scene. 'People have said to me, football must have seemed alien to you, being a woman. But it wasn't: it was the culture, you had to either opt out of that completely and not take any notice of what was happening around you, or you had to take an interest. There were so many strikes in the city, so much unemployment, so many people knocking us, that at least in football, with Liverpool's success in the European Cup, we had something to be proud of.'

But girls existed on the fringes rather than as an integral part of that culture. 'It never occurred to me to actually go to Anfield,' Cathy says. 'It was accepted that boys went to games but girls never, it seemed too macho. To go to a game was a fantasy. I'd pass the ground on a Saturday afternoon and think: "I wish I could be there," but I never considered walking in.'

Football is exclusive. Fathers might automatically take their sons but not think to take their daughters. It is a point Nick Hornby makes: in the early 70s he went to Arsenal with his dad, but 'my sister had to stay at home with her mum and her dolls'. While these barriers are starting to break down in the 1990s, there is still a lingering assumption that women who follow football – with its associations of toughness and maleness – are unfeminine. As football sociologist John Williams puts it: 'Men affirm their masculinity through football; women endanger their femininity.' Hence the cliché that men go to the game and women go shopping. To overcome this barrier many

53

girls have to actively insist on going. As Corinna Merriman says: 'My brother became a Spurs fan quite naturally because my dad took him. But football was important to me, too. It was the first interest that dominated my life. I got to a point where I was so desperate to go that I badgered away at my dad and said: "You've got to take me."'

When fathers do get round to taking their daughters, they can end up being so over-protective that they endanger the joy, the bonding, of the footballing occasion. Just like that old family division over how parents think differently about letting their sons and daughters loose on a Saturday night, it is a change of gendered experience that affects the way we end up living our lives – if we let it get to us. Gillian Howe begged her dad to take her to a Sheffield Wednesday game in the mid-70s but found she did not get quite the same treatment as her brother: 'My brother was allowed to go and stand on the terraces with his mates. But my dad insisted that we get seats – even though I knew he hated sitting – he said it would be too rough for me on the Kop.' While Gillian says she 'liked the fact that her dad was concerned', she also felt it marginalized her fandom – that she was getting special treatment. 'There was an unspoken assumption that women sat down and that the real fans stood. I never felt I was a "proper" fan – that I would get the respect I was due – until I stood on those terraces myself.'

Unlike lads and older men who have grown up with birthday treat trips to the big game, most women fans don't start going to games until they are adults. They often go with a husband, boyfriend or male friend – or as part of a mixed group. In such situations women are liable to be patronized, they are not comfortably considered to be serious fans. As Louise Vacher, a Tottenham supporter of seven years standing, says: 'You end up being a touch cautious in what you say, how you act. You don't unwittingly want to do anything that will mark you out as not a true supporter or as someone going along for the wrong reasons. If you're a woman, there's always going to be speculation that you're there to look at the players' legs or because you're an accessory on the arm of a boyfriend.' Indeed, when Louise bought her season ticket with her friend Will, she felt she had to make it very clear to the supporters around her that he was not her boyfriend. 'I wanted them to know that I had been to my first game before Will, that he was coming with me, actually. I wanted to make it clear that I was not the girlfriend coming along with my boyfriend because this is the only time I get to see him. I do want to be seen as a legitimate supporter in my own right.'

What all these women have in common is that they have successfully overcome the difficulties put in their path to become real, hard-core fans. In so doing, they have glimpsed in the midst of these male codes a game they want to be part of. It is perhaps no surprise then that some of the people best at cherishing football's finest traditions and passing them down through the generations are indeed women just like them.

## Watch with mother

One small but significant group of women are the mothers who take their daughters to games. These mothers know exactly what it's like to be a woman who goes to football. They have had to take the abuse, the sexism, the insults – they have had to fight for their right to be there amongst that mass of men. Now they are going to make damn sure that their daughters aren't put off by those selfsame surface impediments.

'I do my mothering at football,' says Jan Mckenley of taking her daughter Ama and stepdaughter Karla to Arsenal. 'For a woman, going to football is still enough of a novelty for you to get kudos for going. That's what I'm passing on to my daughters.'

'It's made us much closer,' says Sharon Heap of going to Maine Road with her mother Jackie – particularly now that they have established some ground rules. 'My mother was a bit protective at first. When we were in the pub after the game, she would come up and tell me not to drink too much. But we sorted out our differences. I told her: "Don't treat me as your daughter at football, treat me as a friend," so that's what we do, we treat each other as friends.'

In fact, as a result of their shared interest, Jackie says she worries far less about her daughter than she might under other circumstances. It has closed the generation gap. She knows Sharon's friends, because they are her friends too; she doesn't worry who she's out with at night because she knows the people she's with. Even Sharon's boyfriend is a friend of her mother. Karl will often say: 'Is your mother coming out with us?' She has known Karl as long as Sharon has. 'My friends can't believe it,' Sharon says, 'we'll go away for a footballing weekend, and me and Karl will have one

**56**

room and my mother another. And my mates will say: "How can you go for a dirty weekend with your mother?"'

These women are also passing on another message: that women are strong. They are proving to their daughters – by example – that they are not going to let the lads keep them out. If women don't identify with football in quite the same way that men do – they are not there to connect with their deep masculine – they do get something out of being in a minority, a double minority, in that they are both a minority within the crowd and a minority in terms of their feminine peer groups. It's a way of liberating themselves from all those bugbears that a male society has imposed upon them: frailty, vulnerability, a sense of familial responsibility. This feeling of strength – of empowerment – is a dominant theme that runs through many women's accounts of going to football. For the girls who grow up going to football with their mothers, there develops an unspoken coincidence between going to football and being confident in themselves and in their gender. 'I've never consciously thought that I'm strong,' says Sharon Heap, who has been following Manchester City since she was four months old, wrapped in a blanket and held in her mother's arms, 'but I do notice that I'm more confident than the women at work. I won't be pushed around and I'm sure that's connected to football. If you want to get to the toilets at Maine Road you literally have to fight, push and shove your way through a mass of men. You're shouting: "Get out of the way!"'

Nick Hornby describes his own sexual empowerment through football somewhat differently, as 'filling up my trolley in the masculinity supermarket'. What he did not realize at first – it's a comic turn that works well in both the book and film versions of *Fever Pitch* – is that he did not have to pick everything off the shelves, that he could enjoy being part of the crowd without then having to get all hard, run the opposing fans back to the tube station and beat them senseless with broken beer bottles. Men invariably find it easier to pick 'n' mix the parts of the fan psyche they want to adopt, and wilfully reject bits but be aware of them nonetheless. For women it is a whole lot more difficult. We might want to push the barriers back and engage in a bit of puerile banter, sink a few pints, give the other lot a good 'ollering as we sing out for all we're worth but when the banter turns to tits, fannies, cunts and slags, we know who the boys are putting in their place.

## Mind your language

We have not yet reached the stage where women fans are developing their own footballing counterculture. In these times of multiple identities, uncertainty and pluralism, maybe it is no longer even appropriate. But the result is that women, unlike men, rarely find the same kinds of bonding processes through football. Or as Jackie Woodhouse put it in her 1991 National Survey of Female Football Fans: 'The camaraderie associated with being part of a group, especially an all male group, is an essential ingredient of football for many male fans. Females, although they may share in the general feeling of identity with their club, do not seem to have these links with each other, nor indeed express any desire for this.'

In terms of the self-styled, by men, authenticity of 'terrace culture', this is undoubtedly true. But in other, subtler, settings, women can find ways in which football helps to forge an intensity of relationship and affection that no other sports certainly, and precious few other pursuits, are likely to generate. Take one of football's great claims: that it is a common language. It is one of Nick Hornby's key sub-texts, it helps him to get on with his troublesome classroom pupils, to chat easily with their parents, to fit into a new office, to hit it off with film stars, producers, literary editors and the like. If you have got the score that everybody is waiting on, you equip yourself with a whole bunch of new friends in a moment. Almost any fan can tell a tale of how football is a great leveller, breaking down barriers of age, class, gender, rank and race. And it can work for women, too. Jan McKenley, a schools inspector visiting many of the schools Nick Hornby would have passed through as a jobbing English teacher, says that she always wears her Arsenal badge on her inspections. 'It helps me to get into conversations with kids, which is useful when you are trying to assess how they are progressing. They feel I have some empathy with them. And it's true. Me and an eight-year-old are almost equals when talking about football.'

Whether it's being able to have a friendly conversation with the local shopkeeper, buttering up an irate bank manager or using it as a means of easing your way into a new job, football creates a familiarity between people who might otherwise have nothing else in common. As Jan puts it: 'It's not an old boys network or a mafia but there is this sense that I've joined this club called being an Arsenal fan. And when people say: "Are you a serious fan?" I say,

"Yes, I go to matches," and they look back at my proud, black, female face, surprised, but with respect.'

Being knowledgeable about football has been particularly useful for women working in predominantly male occupations. It is a point of entry into a dominant male culture. Naomi Stanford is a personnel manager at a large accountancy firm. Talking about her Saturday afternoons at Millwall's New Den gives her a head start when her fellow senior managers – all men – settle themselves down for a heavy spreadsheeting session.

'Men always seem to start meetings with this bonding device of social chitchat about sport, particularly football. I used to think: "I hope they get this over with quickly, then we can start." But then I realized I could be more participative in the meeting if I could talk about football, so I started supporting my local team, Millwall. Now I can take part in the opening conversational gambit and bonding, and I think it makes me more effective in meetings. I'm not seen quite so much as the lonely outsider,' she explains. As Louise Vacher, head of her own department at a market research company, puts it: 'Men stop looking on you as a woman in a man's situation. They think: "She's a woman but she likes football, so she's one of us."'

However, in order to gain male respect, women often have to over-come an initial barrier. For language is a way of excluding as well as including people. And women have to earn their inclusion in a way men don't. There is an appropriateness about men understanding football – even the man who isn't a serious fan is likely to be allowed to have his say, a courtesy not always extended to women.

The woman who tries to join in the Monday morning post-match analysis is likely, at least to begin with, to be viewed with suspicion. 'The men thought I was trying to spoil their conversation, that I was gabbing about things I knew nothing about,' says Angela Fosdyke of her first attempts to enter the closed male coterie in her office. 'I'd make a valid point but they would just brush it aside. Or I'd try to join in, saying: "I saw that goal," but they simply talked over me.' Angela was determined she was not going to be rendered invisible. 'I took them on,' she says. 'I'd say: "You may not agree with me but I do know what I'm talking about sometimes." And it worked. Once they realized I'm a fan in my own right rather than someone else's girlfriend they included me in the conversation. Now it's automatic.'

Attaining this honorary manhood has also brought problems for Angela. 'Ironically I do feel alienated from the women in my office,' she admits. 'Some of them find my lifestyle completely incomprehensible. We'll have a conversation about what we did over the weekend and I'll say: "I went away," without really thinking about it. There's immediate interest. Was it to see relatives or visit a boyfriend? When I explain it was to watch West Ham that's the end of the discussion. Silence. They can't imagine why a woman in her right mind would want to go to a game.'

Gina Gatland, a pensions supervisor for C&A, receives similar incredulous stares from her female colleagues. 'They think any woman who goes to football must be a bit rough,' she explains. 'It's outrageous, because I wouldn't dream of going to a Tottenham game without washing and blow-drying my hair, doing my make-up and painting my nails.' She thrusts out a pair of neatly manicured peach fingers. Gina is quite convinced that there is no one in her office smarter and better turned out than she is – she knows you can be a football fan and still be feminine.

## Turning the tables

Being given a hard time by the men, and the women, at your workplace is bad enough, but what does a woman do when her partner doesn't share her love for the game? Nick Hornby knew his romantic fate if he confessed too early to a potential girlfriend of his other illicit love: 'Tell a thinking woman you like football and you're in for a pretty sobering glimpse of the female conception of the male.' Or as the posters for *Fever Pitch* the film pithily put it: 'Life gets complicated when you love one woman and worship eleven men.' What happens when the tables are turned – when it's hubby who's left at home and it's the wife who's going home and away, then down the pub for a drink with the boys – and life starts getting not just complicated but topsy-turvy too?

Chris Hodson's partner felt threatened by having to share her affections with Manchester United Football Club. 'He felt I was taking over his masculine role and that made him feel insecure. It was almost as if by being the football fan he thought I was taunting him – saying I'm more of a man than you'll ever be.' Indeed he offered Chris an ultimatum: him or the club. 'He just couldn't bear to think of me on the away coach with 60-odd men: he thought I was there because I wanted to sleep with one of them. He was

62

pathetic.' Needless to say their relationship came to a swift end. But Chris' mother was concerned about her daughter's troubled love life. 'Wouldn't it be better if you took up a hobby more suitable for women?' she asked her daughter. Chris has continued to stand her ground: 'Football's such a beautiful game, why should it just be for men? I'm not going to accept traditional boundary roles. I want a partner who'll respect me enough to support me in all my interests.'

Gina Gatland's husband Dennis said the immortal words: 'Never again,' when she first took him to a Tottenham game just after they were married. 'It was because of me,' she explains. 'He said he'd never been so embarrassed in all his life.' Gina was so sick of the loud and biased Crystal Palace fan behind her – 'who really didn't know what he was talking about' – that she challenged his call for offside. 'I turned round very politely and said: "Don't you realize it's when the ball's played?"' The fan started to argue with Gina who, 'being the typical woman who always has to have the last word', gave as good as she got. Dennis looked on in horror: 'Will you just shut up and stop causing trouble,' he told his wife. 'I'm ashamed to be seen out with you.'

Pat Kirkham recalls being so embarrassed when she finally pers-uaded her non-supporting boyfriend to go along to a Newcastle United match with her in the mid-60s. 'He was very arty and just not engaged with the football culture,' she says, 'and that was very difficult for me. He turned up for the game in his silk bow tie and velvet jacket. I couldn't decide whether I wanted to be seen with him or not.'

Janet Garret is lucky enough to have a partner who shares her passion for football, but she can sympathize with those wives who are left at home by their husbands Saturday after Saturday. 'On the away coach a whole bunch of the men who go are divorced. I can see why, it must be terrible for their partners, football can take up so much of your life.' She adds: 'If I hadn't married a Manchester United fan, I wouldn't have married anyone.' Janet met her husband Jim at Old Trafford: they stood near one another, game in, game out, and gradually got talking. But it took him half a season to pluck up the courage to ask her out, and when he did he picked a most inopportune moment. 'United were just getting close and this massive roar went up from the crowd so I wasn't sure what he'd said. I didn't want to make a fool of myself by saying: "Yes, what time?" So I said: "Pardon?" And he's never let me live that down.' Janet says that football has made her and Jim closer. 'We sit together at games and every other week we spend hours together on the away coach. So we don't drift apart like other couples do – we don't have time to go off and do our own thing. And football is such a broad subject that we've always got something to talk about.'

With football in common, Dave and Kathy McCluggage are like-wise never short of conversation. The trouble is they each follow different teams. 'Different' is putting it mildly: Dave follows lowly Burnley and can hardly bring himself to admit that his wife Kathy is a supporter of their big-time local rivals, Blackburn Rovers. This rivalry may not have quite the superstar status of Celtic and Rangers, Tottenham and Arsenal or Newcastle and Sunderland, but in the old cotton towns of Lancashire it has an intensity that, at times, borders on hatred. Kathy admits: 'When it comes to football we just can't be happy for one another. When his team lose I'm overjoyed, and vice versa,' or as Dave puts it: 'I'd rather go on a Club 18–30 Holiday in Bosnia than go to bloody Blackburn.'

Their rivalry has been intensified by the fact that their teams have undergone such radical reversals of fortune during the course of their marriage. 'When I met Kathy I felt sorry for her,' Dave admits. Burnley were still in what was then the first division while Black-burn were languishing in the fourth. Dave assumed that he would always be the important football fan in their marriage, 'that Burnley would always be bigger and better than Blackburn', that he would continue to smile down on his wife safe in the knowledge that her team was no threat to his. How was he to know that Jack Walker would decide to pump millions into his local club, that Blackburn would climb to the very top of the Premier League while his own team sank rapidly downwards?

Footballing attachments are serious business: they are tied up with feelings of self-worth, pride and status. As Paul, the character representing Hornby in the film of *Fever Pitch*, puts it: 'It all gets

65

mixed up together in your head, and you can't remember whether life's shit because Arsenal are shit or the other way round.' So for Dave to see his own team decline was undoubtedly difficult. At the same time, to see the team of the person closest to him enjoying such unexpected success was unbearable. No wonder, as Kathy admits, they 'can no longer communicate where football's concerned'.

Dave claims he would stop supporting Burnley if they were taken over by a Jack Walker clone. 'Blackburn,' he says, 'have never had their loyalty tested, it's all money, money, money.' Everything he hates about football, the commercialization, the wealth, the wholesale buying in of players, Blackburn represents. Kathy takes a more moderate view: 'I'm pleased we've attracted new supporters – Dave says they're fair weather fans – but some of them will stick with the club even when we stop winning cups.' Indeed the one saving grace, Kathy explains, 'is that Dave knows I'd support Blackburn even if they went back down to the third division,' and adds wryly, 'Football. It's the one thing that stops us getting divorced.'

They do try to be supportive of one another, if only for the sake of family harmony. Take Blackburn's ill-fated foray into Europe in 1995. As Kathy nervously watched Blackburn v Trelleborg on TV, Dave sat by. But when the opposition scored, he couldn't contain himself: 'I rushed out into the kitchen and threw my hands in the air, silently mouthing: "Yes, yes, yes." Then I came out and said: "Cup of tea, dear?"'

When Kathy went to Europe with her club, her fellow supporters found out she had been married to a Burnley fan for 16 years. 'It

66

was like Chinese whispers all round the bus. People came up to me and asked: "Did you know before you married him?", "Did he lie to you?" But they were alright once I explained that we're not friends or anything – that it's just a marriage.'

## Bringing up baby

In any footballing relationship children inevitably become an issue. Nick Hornby wanted his girlfriend to go to football with him – he introduced her to Arsenal. But then he began to wonder where all this chivalry had got him when she suggested: 'Alternate home games I suppose,' during a conversation about children and future childcare arrangements. Hornby was mortified. The very idea that he would have to share Arsenal with his partner, that he would have to stay at home while she sat in his seat, was too much for him to bear, so he set out to prove to her who is the top dog Arsenal fan in their rela- tionship. When he finally wins, he proudly declares: 'When and if we have children, it will be my bottom exclusively that fills our season ticket seat.'

For Debbie Horsfield, playwright and Manchester United fan, it is motherhood that determines the way she is able to support her club. 'I used to be completely obsessed with Manchester United,' she admits. 'I didn't even have a boyfriend until I was 17 because I was more interested in my team. But once you have children your priorities change, you realize there's an appropriateness about putting them first.'

**67**

Debbie believes this is the reason why many female fans drop out of going to games week in week out during the early years of motherhood. 'It's not about being able to get a babysitter or crèche facilities, it's about emotions,' she explains. 'That's why there will never be as many women fans at games as there are men. Women are more domestically oriented in those early years of having children in a way men are not.'

That does not, of course, mean women are not serious about their football. True, it's often the fans who are actively at games week in week out who are considered the genuine article, imbued with real commitment. But what mothers, the elderly, the disabled and the poor know, is that just because they can't physically get to every game it doesn't mean the emotional connection isn't just as strong. Debbie may not have been present at Manchester United when her kids were small but she was never-theless watching on TV or listening on the radio. This idea that you can be a fan in a variety of ways, ranging from being at a game on a wet windy night though to a cosy Sunday afternoon sitting in front of satellite TV is what sociologist Steve Redhead calls post-fandom. It strikes at the heart of a traditional male idea of what it means to be a fan.

In what is sometimes laughingly dubbed the 'choice society' of the late 1990s, we women want to be able to choose what level of fandom we are going to engage in. So if it means alternate games while the kids are growing up, let's negotiate around that, or if a crèche would help out one should be provided, and if we decide following the team from the comfort of our own living rooms is for us until the kids are older, that doesn't make us any less of a fan.

68

It's about having a culture that includes us all as fans, that makes a serious effort to provide the maximum number of ways to attach us to the game, that is what a 'people's game' would be truly all about. Instead, we get the fast-buck marketing mentality that thinks of us all as spend-per-head units on the one hand, or the authenticity warriors in the stands looking down their noses at us for failing to ape their single-minded dedication to the exclusion of everything else.

## Vital statistics

Women fans may, on occasion, have a different relationship to the game, but that is not to say we would give up our right to collect programmes, ground-hop and sup real ale with the best of them. One of the philosophical delights of modern womanhood is we want to have it both ways! Take Coventry City fan Polly Goerres. She spends her football-free weekends visiting one of the 92 league clubs – collecting a memento mug from each stadium she visits of course – and hopes to have entered the austere – and predominantly male – ranks of the 92ers by next year. 'I get a real buzz from going to the grounds,' she admits. 'They're all so different.' Polly has even been known to take in the odd programme fair. 'Please don't make me sound too sad,' she nervously pleads. 'I'd accumulated so many programmes over the years and I couldn't possibly throw them away. So I started to file them neatly away – in their season's binders of course – and I noticed I had some missing.' The programme fair was a bit of an eye-opener. 'I didn't see a single other female collector,' she says, 'but it was the least misogynistic

69

place you could imagine: full of men in cardigans who were so obsessed with finding their programmes they didn't even notice that I was a woman. It's the one place that men aren't precious about their territory.'

For most women, football does still fit somewhere in a scale of priorities, a process that tends to ward off the more extreme ends of obsession that Nick Hornby self-consciously flirts with and denies women can share: 'I have met women who have loved football, and go to watch a number of games a season, but I have yet to meet one who would make that Wednesday night trip to Plymouth… I'm not saying that the anally retentive woman does not exist, but she is vastly outnumbered by her masculine equivalent.' Indeed Freud himself declared men to be the more obsessive sex.

Tottenham supporter Corinna Merriman agrees with Hornby's analysis: 'I consider myself to be pretty obsessive. I rush home to put the teletext on for the match result or transfer gossip. I do all the mental calculations about who is playing who and how many points we need to get out of our next games to qualify for Europe or escape relegation.' But she admits she can't compete with her boyfriend Martin's obsessive knowledge of seasons past, ancient team line-ups, matches won, drawn and lost more than 10 years ago. 'Men seem to be more anal about facts and figures. Men collect – they collect football experiences. I think they are more obsessed with detail but not necessarily with the game, the passion or supporting the team. Women are just as capable of that, we have an emotional commitment.'

But is it more difficult to get the credibility of being a 'proper' fan if you aren't steeped in your club's history? Because football is a predominantly masculine interest, does that mean that if you don't enjoy the sport in the way most men do then you are less of a fan? Helen de Witt is convinced she will never be quite the type of Arsenal fan Nick Hornby is, simply because of her gender: 'All men grow up with this idea that football is intrinsic to their masculinity. Women are excluded from that. You desperately try to make up for lost time by cramming this history into your head, but you can never relive it like men do. They've followed their team from childhood and all those matches are ingrained in their head. Women don't have that.' She wistfully adds: 'And they get so mad if you don't recognize a picture of Liam Brady.'

Is it simply the case that women don't have the necessary background in consuming facts and figures? Kate Norrish, a Chelsea fan, thinks it is: 'Men are more anal in their supporting, judging from my brother. He used to keep his own very sophisticated files of matches and write his own match reports. It was a big part of his life. But on a level of being in the ground there's no difference, I'll shout as loudly as anyone. I've been a competitive sportswoman all my adult life, competing at quite a high level, knowledgeable about how sport works, prepared to comment on tactics and techniques. But with football there's this bizarre, undoubtedly boyish, emphasis on remembering long-past results. Once I'm at the match I can escape all this, I'm anybody's equal and the piss-taking stops. It's about now, not seasons long gone, and for me forgotten.' Helen agreed: 'In the ground all that gendered point-scoring is totally erased, we're all sharing the same thrill of Arsenal winning so sod the statistics.'

## Saturday afternoon passion

Nick Hornby measured his life out through Arsenal fixtures. It gave not only a sense of continuity to a suburban adolescence teetering into middle age but also gave him an escape route, an emotional safety valve where all that pent-up angst could let itself go. And of course when Arsenal won it made up for some of life's other disappointments: 'I had the blues and when I watched my team I could unwrap them and let them breathe a little.' This is what makes football so special, there is simply no other sport that demands, and receives, such a high level of individual attachment. And notwithstanding the TV age we live in there is no obvious sign of this attachment abating.

'Football is completely cathartic. You're on this little island where you don't have to think about anything else. You can burn off a lot of energy. If you want to sing and chant you can and the very act of this is a release. You've got the unpredictability and the excitement. And you've got an oasis in the middle of the rest of your life,' says Debbie Horsfield. It's also an opportunity for Debbie to break out of the responsible convention: 'It's the reversal of my normal situation. I can leave behind my domestic ties, my busy life, my adult responsibilities.'

For Angela Fosdyke, football is a way of finding a side of her personality she never knew she had: she may have to be restrained and respectable at work but: 'I become completely different when I go to West Ham – I feel liberated,' she says. 'You become more aggressive, you get carried away. It's not like you

**72**

have to prove yourself, you don't have to act in a feminine way in front of the people you're with. In fact you forget all about them. It's just you and eleven men and you want to tell them just what you think.' Or as Jan McKenley puts it: 'I don't go to football to be genteel, anything but. I'm an effer and blinder at games.' But she does see some differences between her and other supporters. 'I was once at a game where most of the crowd jumped up and shouted "wanker" at exactly the same time. I wouldn't do that. There are some masculine signals that I don't give.'

Jan believes that the way women support their teams from the stands is different, too. 'I think women are more encouraging. I've never seen a woman walk out. A lot of blokes walk out if Arsenal aren't playing well – maybe they feel it more keenly than women do – but most of the women I see clap, cheer, get behind the team even when we all know they're playing badly.' Angela Forsdyke agrees: 'Maybe it's the softer side of our nature coming out but I do think women are more forgiving. I do get angry and I do shout but I would always give the team the benefit of the doubt. If someone's getting on my nerves I let them know: "Move you tart," but if he then plays better I will praise him. Maybe women are more objective in that sense.'

Perhaps women do have more of a perspective on their fandom: 'I'm told that when I feel sorry for the players when they lose it's the mothering instinct coming out,' says Bolton fan Jean Thomasson. 'You feel for the players, whereas men don't. They only care about whether they win or lose and what the weekend's going to be like if they lose. I've heard men say: "We're going to need oxygen when we get home." Literally, it seems for some men that their whole life has been drained out of them by the failure to win.'

After *Fever Pitch*, almost every club in the country seemed to find its very own soccerati: from Stockport County to Cowdenbeath, Tranmere Rovers to Southampton's Saints. It was as if beneath all those layers of winter clothing donned for the difficult early January cup tie there was an aspiring author waiting to burst forth. In every case the author was a man. Hornby's collection of the new football writing *My Favourite Year* didn't include even a token woman amongst its 13 contributors.

Simon Kuper spearheaded a second wave of writing, still exclusively male, with his 1994 best seller, *Football Against the Enemy*, and has this to say about his Hornbyesque peers: 'Too many books have been written about this sentimental attachment to football on the back of *Fever Pitch*, this idea that I've been following my team for 30 years and my dad did before me and my grandad did before him, that football is about blood and toil and belonging. This is very dangerous for two reasons. First football is about more than belonging and community, it's about art and great moments: George Best beating

74

three defenders down the wing; a Platini free kick. Secondly, it makes Asian fans, black fans, women fans feel excluded. How can you come in if you didn't belong before?'

Kuper is right, women are used to being the object, never the subject, or in more colloquial terms, the bridesmaid, never the bride. Our lives in football rarely make an appearance in these tales, even as objects, let alone as part of football's big happy family. It is not Nick Hornby's fault, the lad didn't do that bad, and in his darker moments he at least faces up to his own inadequacies. But until we are allowed to tell our own tales, until we find that space with the encouragement and support such a space would have to provide, it would be nice if all these enlightened blokes at least recognized that a woman can be just like a fan.

# Saturday's Girls

## Football's Cultural Revolution

Every other Saturday Sally and Lorraine Rooker can be found sitting together in Manchester City's Platt Lane stand. Sally, with her short blonde crop partially hidden by her anorak hood; her daughter Lorraine, arms folded, rubbing her hands against her denim jacket to ward off the cold. Up above the sky is grey and full with rain.

Sitting next to Lorraine is her boyfriend, Craig, and next to him his mates Jim and Shaun. They all go to games together, they are part of the same footballing gang. They were thrust together when Lorraine and Craig met outside the ground, and after he fell in love at first sight, Craig gladly swapped his ticket for one in the same stand as Lorraine, so that he would casually bump into her again. When Lorraine and Craig became an item, his mates changed stands too.

'Football as a setting for romance, you don't often find that,' Lorraine says. There is amazement in her voice that it has happened to her. 'You're so surrounded by blokes at a game, you don't ever have time to think about fancying one of them. We sit on each other's knees with our arms round each other. It's just so innocent. The girls are the same, we hug each other when our team scores. No one goes to football to cop off.'

Craig was shocked at his own feelings. He fiddled with his jacket zip as he spoke. 'My old man's generation, no way would he chat up a woman at a game. Women's place is at home, football is a man's game, so he'd be suspicious about their intentions. But it's different for me and my mates, because loads of women go, and they're just the same as us. No way do we go to meet them but sometimes you can't help but notice a good-looking one. And you don't know what to do. Do you make a move after the game or not? Do you wear your best togs and aftershave and risk your mates having a laugh or do you just forget about it – because it doesn't feel right. I reckon most men go for the last one.'

As Craig admits: 'When you go to football with the lads you do all kinds of things you wouldn't do if you were with a girl. You get tanked up beforehand, have a laugh, probably make a pass at the programme seller, and sing, chant and swear throughout the game. And then you see a woman you fancy. What do you do? Do you carry on and have her think: "What a divvy" – because you know inside what women think about how men act at football. But it can seem like too good an opportunity to miss so you start behaving all grown up.'

If men are in agony deciding how to react to women, women are equally desperate that they shouldn't feel any of that agony because of them. They don't want to disrupt the atmosphere. They go because they love their team and the rowdy, raucous culture that surrounds it. The fact that their non-footballing girlfriends are amazed at tales of late-night drinking sessions and incidents involving police escorts through busy city centres simply adds to the buzz. As Louise Vacher puts it: 'Before I went to football, if anyone had told me I was going to be escorted along a road by a policeman, considered a threat to normal society, I would have said that was very unlikely. But at football it's part of the thrill.' It gives those women a cachet, a way into that perplexing world of men. And it's a subtle form of rebellion, an opportunity for women to behave contrary to what is expected of them. Why on earth would they want to change the rules?'

'One of the reasons I go,' says Helen de Witt, a vivacious Arsenal fan, 'is to be wild, shout and swear, hugging people I've never met before and drinking eight pints afterwards. That's what it's about. It's real participation in the culture as it stands.'

Louise Vacher, a Spurs supporter since 1990, agrees: 'Women don't want to rock the boat, it's not ours to rock. You have respect for those who have committed themselves over years and years. I'm aware that they are people with far more pedigree than me. I'm just pleased they've let me join in.'

## Women with balls

Women fans tend to take their footballing commitments very seriously, precisely because they have a nagging feeling that they are on trial. They have to prove that they know what they are talking about and that they are not just there to ogle the player's bums and legs. 'Women hate the young girls who go to Old Trafford to swoon over Ryan Giggs more than the men do because it perpetuates a stereotype. I wish they would put a bag on his head sometimes,' says long-standing Manchester United fan, Janet Garrett.

Helen de Witt describes her favourite Arsenal player Dennis Bergkamp: 'I do think he's attractive but that's only informed by the fact that he's an Arsenal player. I'm certainly not thinking about his looks during the match, the only balls I'm interested in then are the ones at the back of the net.'

Of her relationship with male fans she admits: 'There is a frisson because you are outnumbered by men about four to one, so it's no surprise if you get chatted up in the pub afterwards, that's just a laugh. But I try to make light of sexual politics. I wear my David Seaman shirt and wait for the first bloke to say: "Oy, you've got 'semen' on your shirt." I don't find that offensive. It's an acceptance of our differences.'

In fact the majority of female fans see football as a place remarkably free from sexual overtones, surprisingly, considering its predominantly masculine nature. Jenny Downs, 28 and a West Ham supporter, says that she has 'never felt intimidated at football. Men are going to football with their mates, they are not going on the pull, if it was a nightclub situation it would be totally different. But they are ordering their lives in a certain way: pub, football, home, bath, clubbing. The only time I've been eyed up is by the away supporters – maybe their priorities are a bit different. Once you become a fan you become one of us, one of the lads.'

It is the women who aren't at the ground as fans who bear the brunt of sexual innuendo. Linda Youell worked as a steward at Millwall football club but she is also an Everton fan. When she attends Everton games she is simply a fan and that fandom gives her a measure of protection from sexual insult that she does not receive when she puts on her Millwall steward's bib and becomes an official of the club.

Linda has had to sit facing fifty boozy blokes singing: 'Get your tits out for the lads.' 'It was horrible, I did feel intimidated. After the game I went up to a couple of the blokes and asked them why they did that. I told them I was a hard-up student trying to make some extra cash. They were shocked that I was upset. "Sorry love, we didn't mean anything by it. It's just the lads having a laugh." I would hope in future that they might think twice, but I doubt it. They like to show off to their mates and that makes them behave in a way they wouldn't do if they were on their own.'

John Williams of the Sir Norman Chester Centre for Football Research puts this unacceptable behaviour down to the way some men want to bond with other men at football: 'Many want to be overtly sexist and racist. They need to have this exaggerated sense of their sexuality to defend themselves from potential accusations that they are not really men. English men are very unsure of their sexual identities and, consequently, have to reaffirm themselves as real men by talking about women in a way that is derogatory to women and derogatory to men. Much of male bonding is conversations around this core.'

81

But not all men are the same. At least some men have grown up with the idea that men and women are equal. They may be surprised to find women at games but that does not mean that they feel threatened by it. Lorraine's boyfriend Craig is by no means a new man; he works as a mechanic in a traditionally male atmosphere and enjoys a bevvy with the lads. But he believes that meeting Lorraine and going to football with her has changed his opinion of women. 'We have a real laugh together – she doesn't behave how I expected women to behave, you know, checking to see if you've had too much to drink or what you're spending your money on.' And he admits that it has changed his view of how men should behave. Once he never questioned the right of any man to make fun of a female football fan and laughed along with the usual jibes – 'Do you know which way the team's playing love?', 'Women don't really understand the game, they've never played.' 'But now when I hear lads taking the piss out of them, or whistling at the programme sellers it pisses me off – it could be my girlfriend they are having a go at.'

The fact that more women are now visible at games has also brought with it an unwelcome gender tension. Football writer Julie Welch explains it thus: 'Football is a closed male world and men feel self-conscious if there's a woman there. And I sympathize, because when I go to my aerobics class and there are these two huge blokes in this room full of women, we really don't want them there. It's a physical feeling, you can't quite be the gender being you want to be if there's someone of the opposite sex there. But we've got to live with it, men are going to go to aerobics and women are going to go to football.'

82

Men like Craig are man enough to deal with this tension. They are beginning to recognize that men don't own football. But it does take some getting used to. Not all men approve. They would rather not only football but the world hadn't changed. For more women at games is a sign of the growing independence of women, their increasing economic wealth and the breakdown of traditional roles – the idea that men went to work and football while women stayed at home and looked after the kids. No wonder they claim that women are not really true fans but there to ogle the players' legs and bums.

Of course some women, and girls in particular, do have crushes on players. It was in teenage magazines that girls first began to see pin-ups and interviews with the likes of George Best, Glenn Hoddle and Kevin Keegan. In recent times it has just mushroomed with star players like David Ginola, Jamie Redknapp and Trevor Sinclair appearing in style magazines, on the catwalk, and in the case of Spurs goalkeeper Ian Walker, as a male centrefold. While for many years female athletes have been presented in overtly sexual terms, it is only in the last five years that male athletes have become objects of the female gaze.

## Get your kit off for the lasses

Undoubtedly these images have made some women more aware of football but has it given them the impetus to go? 'For me it was a combination of things says,' Jane Greenham, a 22-year-old Queens Park Rangers fan. 'I don't come from a footballing family, so seeing

83

a picture of Ryan Giggs in a magazine was my first introduction to football. I'd always thought of footballers as hard and hairy but he was just gorgeous. And it did spark my interest, so when I was asked to go to a QPR game I said yes. Now I'm a season ticket holder. And yes I do like Trevor Sinclair but it's because of his skill as much as his looks. But you would never shout anything sexy at a player, it's just not cool to publicly fancy them.'

Is fancying players something to feel ashamed of? 'Certainly not,' says former music journalist and now artist, Caroline Coon: 'I'm always mystified why the whole audience at football isn't women. Part of the thrill is seeing very beautiful, half-naked men pit themselves to the optimum of their physicality. That is as much a part of football as the skill factor.'

But girls soon learn that men don't like women bringing sex into football, as Corinna Merriman well remembers. She and her teenage friends went to see Spurs play Coventry with her brother who was a couple of years older. 'Coventry had a corner. Glenn Hoddle was in the box and we were behind the goal. And one of my friends shouted: "Glenn, Glenn, I love you." My brother was dying on the spot. Glenn turned round to look, Coventry took the corner and scored. My brother was furious: "It's all your fault they've scored." He determined never again to go with girls to football because they ruined the game.'

It may be that men are afraid to show their feelings, to admit that they have crushes on their favourite players too. Caroline Coon offers this analysis: 'I don't think the guys could go to football and

84

salivate over the prowess of the players without a homoerotic play there. It's just that they don't acknowledge it.' But perhaps that is beginning to change too: in the height of passion, men routinely refer to loving players, describing a sensational goal as better than sex, and even crying. It's an area where some men can release emotions traditionally associated with being female. Perhaps they feel uneasy at seeing women watching them do this.

Men do become obsessed with their favourite players but in a different way. They dream about becoming professional football players. For women until very recently being a female football player almost seemed like a contradiction in terms. There were no role models. No wonder then that for so many young girls their only route into football, in terms of having a fantasy about it, was to be a footballer's girlfriend.

Vanessa Price, 23 and an Everton fan, was obsessed with the club's star striker Graham Sharp in her teens: she knew the street he lived on, what clubs he went out to at night – even where he went shopping and on what day. Now studying for an MA in psychology, she says that some of the male supporters are jealous of the attention their heroes get from women. 'It's about male competition. They can't compete, because most fans haven't got the players' bodies, money or the status. They don't blame the players because they are their heroes, so they blame women for bringing sex into it.' But she explains, 'It wasn't even so much about sex, I was shy of boys at 13, it was about companionship. Going with your best mate to the ground and screaming and shouting at your favourite player. Losing yourself in something exciting but ultimately safe, because deep down you know nothing will come of it. If Graham Sharp had propositioned me I would have run a mile.' There would be some who would dismiss Vanessa as not a true Everton supporter but that would be unfair because she still follows her team week in week out. There will be female 'groupies' for as long as women are taught to value themselves by the status of their men. It's about wanting to get fame and recognition by waiting for a man to provide it, rather than going and getting it for yourself. While the great strides that are being made in women's football are to be congratulated – a whole generation of women need never have to suffer the put-down that you can't understand football because you've never played – it will not alter the basic point that women can still fantasize about marrying the players and men can't.

## The manners police

Manners don't just govern sexual relations. There is an assumption that women and men have different codes of behaviour, different standards about what constitutes good and bad. Women are assumed to be less aggressive, more passive, more caring than men. In terms of football this means they are more likely to want to sit down, less likely to swear and less likely to put up with some of the antics that men pass off as just a bit of the bonding process. Women with their strategically timed frowns and scowls can curb the fervour of any excitable bloke; their astonished tuts will have the more cautious man looking round to check whether it's safe to swear, and their desire not to be too close to these flaying figures of manhood as they sweep en masse across the terraces at the first whiff of a goal makes seats the ideal solution.

This is the idea that women can be a civilizing influence on men. 'Civilizing' – it's an idea that makes your average female fan sick with disgust. They go to games to enjoy the football just like any other fan. They don't want to act as informal manners police. It may well be true that if more women went to games it would have an effect on the way men behave. But that isn't why women go. And it would hardly make football appealing to women if they believed they were responsible, just because they are women, for maintaining the moral standards of the game. It's hard enough for women to prove themselves as fans without being sectioned off for special duties.

Editor of *Shoot* Eleanor Levy says: 'Most women who like football hate the fact that they are women being focused on too much. At Tottenham they have signs up where I sit: "This is a family stand. There are women and children present, please mind your language." This really grates because the one thing I don't want as a football fan is the bloke in front of me resenting me being here because he thinks he can't swear.'

This idea that women could change the culture of football gained prominence in the aftermath of the Hillsborough stadium disaster where 96 fans were crushed to death. This tragedy forced supporters, administrators and planners to have a long, hard look at what was wrong with the game. Dangerous stadia, out-of-date facilities and a propensity towards violence on the part of a minority of male supporters were identified as the three big problems. The solution: a new image for football including all-seater stadia, better facilities and a new audience, of which women, given their supposedly caring nature, would be an ideal component, to offset the aggressive characteristics of the masculine horde.

Football's women felt patronized. They want to be a valid part of the environment as it is, not there to clean up football's supposedly 'sordid' act. Take Caroline Coon, who first started going to football in the 1960s and was instantly gripped by the absolute maleness of it all: 'I liked the fact that I was going into the heart of working class, patriarchal culture. It was like entering forbidden territory. I really had to watch my back, be calm enough to take the insults and be as strong as the boys.' For Caroline, football was a way of proving to herself that women can be 'as randy, as drunk, as obscene as men. It was an affirmation that gender difference was social.'

## Do you want to be in my gang?

After a hard-fought 1–1 draw with Spurs, Lorraine and Sally Rooker certainly like to feel they have successfully invaded Caroline Coon's 'forbidden territory'. Sally was sitting at a corner table with four of the lads. Pints all round. The City fans were in a good mood. It was the start of a new season and they hadn't lost. Craig and three of his mates were having a mini football match in the middle of the room using a scrunched up poster of Eric Cantona (found behind one of the seats) as the football. It is headed to Lorraine who has suddenly been recruited as the goalkeeper. She saves it, to cries of 'Go Coton!'

'I wouldn't have ever imagined my mum looking on while I act the fool in the middle of the pub,' Lorraine laughed. 'But that's what is so great about football. We can be part of this tremendous atmosphere. It's like learning to do all kinds of things that women wouldn't normally do – be raucous and wild. And somehow it's acceptable because you become an honorary bloke.'

The conversation is light-hearted, witty, clever, acerbic, but not exactly deep. It is lads' talk. And that's why these women like it. 'It's different to a night out with the girls,' says Lorraine, 'because all you talk about is football. If you are out with the girls you'll have a good giggle but you also end up yakking about serious stuff like men, work and relationships. With the lads you can get away from that completely.' Football is serious precisely because it is an opportunity to get emotional and completely involved in something that, at the end of the day, is not the most important thing in life.

Craig and his pals were apt to start up at any time a chant: 'City, the only team from Manchester,' or simply 'City, City, City,' each word being interspersed with a loud clap. Be it in the pub, down the road, in the chip shop, the chant was a unifier for the men. Glasses would come clashing together in the pub as arms were raised in salute to 'the greatest team in the world'; chips were thrown in the air (and at the 'old lad, pissed as a newt' who was meandering a mite worse for wear down the street) as the gang

89

walked from the chip shop in the direction of town awash with boozy banter. In the midst of all this was Lorraine – singing, shouting, swaying. No longer the lone woman but one of the gang. 'I feel like I belong,' she uttered the words with pride, 'and that makes me feel special. I've earned my right to be part of the gang. It's like seeing what makes men tick, looking into a world you used to wonder about before. I certainly don't have any illusions about men anymore. I'm as good or as bad as any one of them.'

'I don't get so angry with the players when we have a bad game. I can get pissed off and moody for days but I don't hate o ur players when they've let us down like Craig does, I just feel sad,' Lorraine said when asked about the differences between how she and her boyfriend relate to football. While plenty of men will also cry at football and feel sad and dejected – it is rarer for women to feel the kind of anger that some men display when they lose. 'They take defeat so personally, as if it's an insult to them, to their honour,' says Jean Thomasson, 62, a long-standing Bolton supporter. 'One Bolton fan burned his season ticket in the middle of the pub because the team looked like being relegated. He decided they no longer deserved his support. Even my son-in-law, he'll be at a game and if a player misses a pass he'll get all steamed up and say: "If I played like that at for my Sunday League club I'd be out." As if he's ever likely to play in the Premier or Nationwide League.

'For me, loyalty is about getting things in proportion. I don't fly off the handle at the first defeat but try to imagine what it must be like

for the players, how bad they must feel. And that makes you more
determined to be there next week. I don't go home and sulk, like
my dad used to do. Why should I be miserable? I've been coming
since Bolton were in the fourth division. They're in the Premier
League now.'

Neither do the majority of women feel the same need to stake
out their territory that some men do. As Gillian Howe says: 'I've
seen groups of lads at Sheffield Wednesday games, jeering and
taunting the opposing team in very strong language, telling them
to fuck off back to the shit hole they came from. I passionately
want my team to win and I don't like the opposing team, I'm
all for calling their players "donkey" and what have you. But
I'm not sure I feel so strongly that kind of hate, almost, of other
supporters. I don't feel they've invaded my territory in quite the
way some men do.' But she adds: 'When I go to away games I
do get a bit of a sense of that. If you have a police escort, it feels
very dramatic and intense, so I do understand how some of those
men feel.'

saturday's girls: football's cultural revolution

Jonathan Rutherford, a writer on masculinity, says: 'Football brings out infantile forms of identification, clear polarizations between us and them. It's like a form of ethnic cleansing on the terraces. There's something about the collective male psyche that seems to want it, need it, take pleasure in it.' One of the reasons some men don't like women – or indeed anyone who is different to themselves – to be there, is that they feel they can't bond in quite that same way. The audience is no longer simply full of men like themselves who get that same thrill. The ground is no longer polarized in terms of two invading rival groups, it is more diverse. But, as John Williams says, it's not simply that there is a more diverse audience, which has forced a debate about what good behaviour constitutes at a football ground. With the change to all-seater stadia, 'the self-segregation of parts of the stadia are gone'. It is no longer possible for groups of men who want to express themselves in that way to stand together.

In an age where the level of female aggression is reported to be on the increase, cases of male battering are hitting the headlines and female tag-posses are not an uncommon sight on city streets late at night, it might be expected that a younger generation of women would be involved in some of the fracas that take place around football. But this doesn't appear to be the case. Because of changes in policing at games and youth culture, football is no longer the obvious place to go, either to prove your toughness or to get into a fight. Young women today who are involved in crime are far more likely to be in the drugs scene, shoplifting or mugging than getting into fights at football.

If gangs of women don't go to games looking for trouble, that is not to say that female fans aren't prepared to be violent if it means helping someone they care about. 'If anyone hit one of the lads in our gang, I'd jump in and defend them,' said Sharon Heap. 'You speak up for your own. I don't go looking for a fight but I would get stuck in if I had to.'

Women generally do have a completely different view of violence. Plenty of women fans have seen fights but they have always been between groups of men. Women tend to feel that as long as they get out of the way they will be safe. There is no kudos to be gained from hitting a member of the 'weaker' sex – be it woman or child. As Liverpool fan Shiela Spiers says: 'All men of whatever age realize they could be prey to violence. And that makes them much more wary and prepared than women. The few times I've taken off my colours it's always been because some man has told me to: he was aware that there might be trouble whereas I was totally unaware it could happen to me.'

## Safety measures

In some ways perhaps women are safer at football – even during the 1970s and 80s – than men, because amongst the fans there is such a strong social stigma attached to attacking women. It may even give women more freedom to speak their minds. At home it's another matter, Gazza certainly won't have been the first player, fan or manager to beat up his wife or girlfriend. But in front of your mates you're hardly proving how hard you are by piling into the

93

away fan's girlfriends and mothers. The lads have tougher fish to fry. This is where women as the civilizing influence does kick in. Even if women don't wish to be seen in those terms, their presence can have an effect on male behaviour.

Pat Smith, deputy chief executive of the Football Association, swears that having a woman in charge of ticketing saved the day during Italia 90. 'I took my team out to Italy to run the ticketing. We had two aggressive days with supporters expecting to get tickets for England's semi-final against Germany there and then. I staffed the main stand with a woman and it was our salvation because if it had been a man running it the supporters would have tried to come over the top. With a woman a sixth sense tells them to hold back fractionally.'

It is as much cultural as anything women do. As Manchester City fan Sue Wallis says: 'If a couple of blokes are arguing in the stand and spoiling the game for everyone else, I will tell them to shut up. Women fans are able to speak for the rest of the supporters, including men who would like to say something but don't dare. For a man to do that would be much harder, it would mean that the person he spoke to would have to retaliate in some way.'

This is something that Jenny Downs knows well. A West Ham supporter, Jenny is a prime example of how women can begin to change the culture of football in a way that would be more difficult for men. Jenny finds racism disgusting and rather than deciding to stay quiet when she hears insults, she tackles them head on.

94

She began going to West Ham in 1988. 'I heard this man behind me start to shout racist abuse at one of the players so I told him: "I don't pay to come to football to listen to this."' The man was stunned. He started to swear at her, and said to her boyfriend: 'Can't you keep your missus in order?' At which point Jenny told him she was going to find a steward who would eject him from the ground.

But finding a sympathetic steward proved difficult. One claimed not to have heard anything. Another asked: 'What the fuck do you expect me to do about it?' Jenny insisted he eject the supporter from the ground. Sadly, other members of the crowd were angered by her action: she was telling tales on one of her own. With no one prepared to help her, Jenny informed a policeman. His response? 'Don't you think you are a little over-excited?' When she finally returned to the stand the offending man had moved which Jenny took as an indication that a small victory had been scored – even if she had missed half the game in the process. And during the rest of the game she had to put up with 'you slag' every time she cheered the team.

'West Ham fans can be very kind. It's one big happy family. If a kid was in danger they'd pass him over their heads to safety. But how big is that family? Does it include women or black people?' Jenny thinks not. She would like West Ham to attract a more diverse audience: one that includes the surrounding community's large ethnic population. Jenny feels part of the problem lies with the image of the club's current captain, classic defensive hard-man Julian Dicks, and the vociferous support given to his misdemeanours by a large section of West Ham's most loyal fans. 'What sort of impression does Dicks give to the outside world? He's a thug. He should leave before he seriously injures someone. And then you have the supporters who idolize him and think it's acceptable to be tough, just like Dicks, off the pitch. When they come teeming out of the ground, shouting and jeering en masse, no wonder people think: "I don't want anything to do with this." I've thought it myself, then I think: "Why should I be forced out?" That would be letting these yobs win.'

## Makeover time

There has been some progress in achieving the more diverse audience at football games that Jenny wants to see. In particular, more women are undoubtedly going to games. But this change has in part been resented by some of the more traditional supporters – women included. For the rising number of women fans represents a broader process of unwelcome change that is on occasion dramatically and critically dubbed 'the death of football'.

Many women didn't go to games during the 1970s and 80s because of football's associations with hooliganism. A whole generation of children – boys and girls – missed out on live football because their parents refused to let them go to games for fear of the terrors that lurked inside football stadia. Those women that did go have memories of a place that was far from welcoming. Kate Norrish remembers going to Chelsea during the 70s and seeing the boot boys selling the National Front's youth paper, *British Bulldog*, outside Stamford Bridge. 'And when you went into the ground you would see rows and rows of Doctor Marten boots and shoe laces hanging up. The police made anyone wearing heavy shoes take them off.' Going to the toilets was a nightmare. Kate says that at Chelsea the only women's toilet was a grubby affair housed in a rickety makeshift shed. 'The only consolation was that there were so few women, at least there was never a queue.'

Sue Wallis remembers going to Manchester City and seeing rows of men peeing up against the inside wall. 'I had my young son with me. What sort of example is that to set a child?' And, of course, there are countless women who could only imagine what was happening on the pitch. Louise Vacher says she used to watch *Match of the Day* after going to a game and think: 'Oh, that's how the goal happened,' because she just could not see over the heads of the other supporters.

Radio 5 Live sports reporter Eleanor Oldroyd, who supported Birmingham City as a child, says she has 'no great nostalgia for the terraces'. She stopped going in the late 70s because the violence got so bad. 'I remember one game, Aston Villa v Birmingham, that was really horrible. Everyone kept surging forward and I was practically trampled. I ended up standing on a wall, clinging to a fence. I was so frightened.'

In that sense, the stadium changes have been beneficial for women. As Gill Bridge, managing director of Blackpool says: 'A safer environment and better facilities have attracted more women.

**97**

It provides a welcoming environment. No woman wants to go to an army camp, complete with grill fences. But that's what football was like. And women did find it threatening.'

Undoubtedly stadia are safer places and less violent than three years ago and sociologist John Williams says that is in part down to women. 'Having women in spaces that have previously been sanctioned as male spaces does change how men think about the spaces they inhabit and what sort of behaviour is required in these spaces.'

It was not just women who were attracted to football in the light of these changes, but men too. That it happened at just the same time as Italia 90, a spectacle of football that was watched by 28 million people – half of them women – brought renewed interest from all quarters. Football had again become a national event. At the same time, fans were organizing through-out the fanzine movement and supporters' associations to clean up the image of football. Suddenly it was hip to be a football supporter again.

Football marketing managers have undoubtedly been out to attract a new type of affluent fan. High prices have made it difficult for some of the traditional supporters to go to games. But that is not the fault of women. Football should be inclusive, a sport for everyone and that includes women but also black fans, disabled fans and poor fans. It can only be truly inclusive if it is affordable for all. That it isn't is due to the way football has changed since 1990, to the way in which football has become big business.

Of course, many supporters do not like these changes. And that goes for some women fans too. As sociologist John Williams says: 'The problem for female fans is that in the minds of many men they are strongly associated with the new tradition that's about marketing and casual support. There's an idea that the game has shifted to suit them. Women who've been going to games for a long time instinctively feel they have to be in the luddite camp because they are being blamed for the changes. They feel forced to say: "We don't want things to change, don't blame us chaps."'

There is a great nostalgia amongst such fans for the terraces of old. But as sociologist Ian Taylor has suggested, people who defend the terraces are really remembering the terraces of the 50s and 60s, not those of the 70s and 80s. They forget that much of terrace culture is violent, racist, sexist and far from witty. And there is a disdain for this 'middle class takeover': the idea that not only have prices shot up but football has lost the very thing that made it special, that earthy, gritty experience which was part of

99

its appeal. It has been civilized. It is as if one has to either love all the changes that have happened post 1990 or you have to hate them all, that you have to defend the terrible lack of facilities, the lack of safety and the racism of the old days.

But for John Williams, the complaints from the traditional male fan about the high prices and middle class takeover are really an attack on women fans: 'They connect the attendance of women with a loss of intensity. Even those who say they don't want hooliganism, they do want that frisson, that intensity of rivalry. Can you have the intensity without that other thing that went with it ? No.'

He goes on to say: 'Complaints from the traditional male fans about the game's new terracotta armies are couched in terms which imply the class roots of the sport have been betrayed by the advent of a new affluent audience for the game seduced less by the sport than by its branded duvets and cuddly toys. But aren't these really complaints that football culture in England over the past few years has been unacceptably feminized?'

Feminization undoubtedly softens football's odd 'rough edge', but to lumber all women with this weighty responsibility to 'civilize' is unfair and by and large unwanted. There might not be many women 'firms' but in most other respects there are as many different types of women going to football as there are women. Women in anoraks with programme collecting on their minds; some tanked up after a lager-guzzling binge; a dutiful girlfriend or a woman out to cop off with that fringed dreamboat

**100**

in row C. Women might be different from men but they are also different from each other. So one woman's idea of what is civilized behaviour will be another's censorship. There is no single 'position' or view-point that encompasses all women. And that means that at last women can think of themselves as fans, not as intruders.

# Home and Away

## Stories of Players' Wives

From the Brylcreemed golden boys of the 50s – Stanley Matthews, Tom Finney, Billy Wright and the like – to the golden age splendour of West Ham's World Cup winning trio Bobby Moore, Geoff Hurst and Martin Peters, or the 70s flair-playing mavericks like George Best, Rodney Marsh and Frank Worthington, football is awash with nostalgia. Back then the game always seemed to be bathed in a better light. Whether it's the pre-Premiership whiff of dogged authenticity, or the days when English football ruled the world, or the unbridled creativity of players who led a truly rebellious life, football's fans are always looking for one benchmark or other against which to measure the present. The new technology of computer generated images coupled with the burgeoning industry in golden oldies replica kits means these past lives are very much part of our footballing present. Magazines, books, late night TV action replays of long-forgotten 70s highlights are all helping to fuel this process. That women fans of yesteryear are absent from these flickering pictures and sepia tints is one way in which men can assert that this history belongs to them, even if tomorrow it no longer does. Another process is to treat these great heroes, for that is what they remain for all fans, in masculine isolation. But the wives, mothers, daughters and girlfriends who in their awkwardness occasionally elbow their way into the frame, are part and parcel of the process that enabled these men to become the great players and managers they undoubtedly were.

In the modern media age we know a whole lot more about the lives of our heroes. They are no longer present just on the back pages of the newspapers, but on the front and in the middle too. England international Teddy Sheringham appeared with his girlfriend on the cover of *Hello* magazine, Lorraine Merson wrote a chapter in her husband's autobiography, Gary and Michelle Lineker took up countless tabloid column inches when their son contracted leukaemia. Whereas once football's secrets were hushed up, now they are exposed: we know about Tony Adams' drink problem, Paul Merson's cocaine addiction, Paul Gascoigne's violent temper. Through the media we have a better picture of what the modern footballer's life is like.

In comparison, we still know very little about the domestic, emotional and familial infrastructure that surrounded the on-field exploits of the stars of the 1960s and 70s. Yet these players are held up as representative of their age. Without the other side of the story, we can't understand that golden age. It will remain forever rose-tinted.

## Lorraine Astle – the King and I

'Jeff, you need to get your blue shirt and dark blue slacks from the car,' Lorraine Astle tells her husband. 'I've pressed them ready for you to put on.' Jeff trots off meekly. But Lorraine can't settle until he's back, mission accomplished, clothes in hand. 'I always worry he'll drop them in a puddle,' she smiles. 'That's footballers for you.'

Lorraine and I were sitting in Jeff Astle's dressing room – complete with star on the door – at the *Fantasy Football* studios in south London. Jeff, a footballing hero to legions of West Bromwich Albion fans, including *Fantasy Football* presenter Frank Skinner, has in the 1990s been reborn as a football legend-cum-singer.

Lorraine is there right behind him – making sure his tie is straight, 'Has he got his song sheet?', 'Does he know he's on the set at 3 p.m.?' – just as she always has been ever since they married in 1963. Back then Jeff earned £12 a week as a centre forward for third division Notts County. 'It certainly wasn't glamorous to marry a footballer back then,' Lorraine laughs. Jeff may have gone on to bigger and better footballing achievements – including playing for England – but one thing remains the same: he couldn't have come this far without the support of his wife.

Jeff may be visible on the TV but what we don't see is Lorraine in the background. On the set of *Fantasy Football* Lorraine stood just off camera. Headphones on, her face still with concentration, as she listened for the first strains of music to come through, and when it did, she beat her hands in time to the music. Jeff stood on camera, watching his wife, waiting for her to point at him, his cue to start singing.

'I like to take a background role,' Lorraine says of their partnership. 'That way I can take a wider scope – I can stand back, make sure no one's making a fool of Jeff.' She says that it's often very hard for footballers to get a handle on their own fame, they need someone both to look out for them – think of all those footballers who have lost money in dodgy business ventures – and keep their feet on the ground. 'Footballers have egos – any wife will tell you that. They are used to people fawning all over them, telling them how great they are, and sometimes they can step out of reality and into a fantasy land. They need someone in the background saying: "Whoa, hold on, don't believe your own hype."' The players that don't have someone – usually a wife – to keep their feet on the ground are the ones that go astray. As Lorraine puts it: 'If George Best had had someone to say: "You're going over the top," he wouldn't have ended up the way he did.'

While managers such as Brian Clough might enjoy downplaying their importance – he has said: 'Wives should be like small children, seen but not heard' – they are the great unsung heroes of football. They have traditionally provided a stable home environment so that their husbands can retain the single-mindedness they need to perform on the pitch. But they get so little credit for doing this – from football clubs at least.

Brian Clough, again, declared that he liked his players to be married – 'It quietens them [the players] down,' but he did not expect wives to get above themselves, to dare to make comments on club decisions. As Janine Self, sportswriter on the *Sun*, puts it: 'Football clubs see wives as appendages, but necessary appendages.'

**106**

It's a point Lorraine agrees with. 'The club liked wives to keep quiet, and in truth I was quite happy to do that. But then what choice do you have when the club is your livelihood?' There were times when she was tempted to tell Jeff: 'I wouldn't do that if I were you,' but she held back. 'Clubs expect wives to leave the major decisions to them.' She prefers the role she has now that Jeff is retired from football: 'I'm in much better position to tell him what I think.'

The lowly position of wives in the footballing hierarchy has finally reached centre stage via Paul Gascoigne's alleged beating of his wife Sheryl. When a cowardly football establishment claims that what goes on behind closed doors is none of its affair, it speaks volumes about the value attributed to wives. As journalist Suzanne Moore puts it, while Gascoigne 'would be banned [from the England squad] for taking recreational drugs, wife-beating is not considered a serious enough incident. The message is clear: the game is more important than anything else; winning is everything.'

But perhaps the tables are turning. Martin Jacques, writing in the *Guardian*, sees the fact that the issue has been raised at all as evidence of a new emphasis on morality. 'It was inconceivable that even 10 years ago that would have been considered as grounds for excluding a player from the England team, that bastion of traditional masculinity: it would have been hushed up... When Gazza said he could not criticize the women's groups that had been campaigning against his selection, it spoke of a transformation in the balance of power within our culture.'

It's not just moral pressure that is being placed on the football establishment to clean up its act and adapt to the modern age. A new generation of players' partners are refusing to do what their contemporaries did in the 1960s and put their husband's careers first. They expect to have careers too. They may well be far less willing to bow to the dictates of some club manager.

In 1996, Claire Gardener, the girlfriend of QPR's star striker Daniele Dichio, for example, revealed in *Arena* magazine that she had started on an interior design course at London Guildhall University. 'I hate the idea of being supported by Dani,' she says. 'I've got to put my life first. I'm not sitting at home waiting for him to play football once a week.' And if that means not moving with him, should he be transferred to the other side of the country while she is undertaking her course, then so be it. Ironically, just a year later, the talk was of Dichio going to the Italian side Sampadoria. Claire may have to make choices she never dreamed of.

But if these aspirations were not those of players' wives in the 60s, it should not imply that they were not independent. They were, but in a different way. As Lorraine says, running a home single-handedly – 'Jeff has always left everything to me' – meant, ironically, that she felt more independent than most of her female peers.

'Friends have said to me: "If my husband was away, I wouldn't know how to pay a bill." I'm horrified at that, to leave every mortal thing to your husband. Perhaps some women like their husbands to take control. I wouldn't like that at all.'

Wives during the 1960s – and a good many today – may have lacked the financial independence that comes from having a career, but they were certainly not emotionally dependent on their husbands – too often they were simply not around. 'You have to be able to cope by yourself,' Lorraine says, 'otherwise every time your husband went through the door, you'd be asking: "Where are you going?", "What time will you be back?" And that's when the trouble starts.'

Lorraine got used to Jeff being away for long periods. 'Although I hated it, it seemed like a lifetime,' she accepted it. Jeff would go away for six weeks at a time, when West Brom went on tour at the end of the football season. Wives were not invited, even though it was considered an opportunity for the team to relax after a hard season. In Jeff's case, he was away more than many other players because he was regularly selected for England tours too.

What Lorraine didn't like was the intrusion Jeff's absences made on their family life – a reason why now Jeff has retired, she is determined he finds time to see their grandchildren. 'I remember once Jeff went on tour and our daughter wasn't walking when he left. He came back six weeks later and she toddled towards him at the airport. I was so sad that he'd missed her taking her first steps.'

'Players' wives have to be patient,' says Rachel Anderson, the only female registered agent in England and whose clients include West Ham hard-man Julian Dicks. 'Football clubs have itineraries that they change at very short notice. A player may have been planning a family outing but what happens? Suddenly he can't go because he has to train, or there's a last minute game. And it's the wife who has to pick up the pieces. She has to explain to a tearful child that Daddy won't be able to go with them after all. It's no wonder players' wives snap and say: "Who's more important, me or the club?"'

She believes there are many simple practical steps clubs could take to support wives, not just in terms of sorting out their itineraries sooner. 'Football clubs could be much more family friendly. When a player moves to a new club, why don't they have lists of local estate agents, schools and other amenities? This would help wives new to an area – where they generally know no one – to settle in. If a player likes golf or fishing, for instance, why don't clubs provide information on residential areas close to their chosen interest? It's those little things that make a difference.'

Transfers are very stressful for wives – not least because they are usually the last to know about them. Claire Ince was criticized by the Italian tabloids because she was unsure about whether her husband Paul should accept a £7 million transfer to Inter Milan. What was she fussing about? Trivial problems like finding a good school for their son and a house the family could be comfortable in. In the opening months of the 1996–7 season, Brazilian ace Emerson walked out on Middlesbrough football club because his wife Andrea was homesick. 'My wife has found it impossible to come to terms with life in Middlesbrough. She has spent much of the last month in tears which, of course, has made me extremely upset,' he told the *Sun*. While in this instance Emerson and Andrea did return to Middlesbrough, it does illustrate that wives' views can't simply be dismissed in transfer negotiations. If a footballer's wife is unhappy it affects him, and ultimately the smooth-running of the club. As Lorraine puts it: 'Clubs should consult wives over transfers. If a wife doesn't want to move, what is the point in that player going? It just causes upset. If a player moves to a new club and his wife stays put, he won't settle. And the manager won't have got a player who is playing as well as he can, so it will just rebound in his face.'

## Carol Worthington – frank about Frank

Frank Worthington was one of football's rebels. In the 1970s English football was an intensely physical game, the nicknames Ron 'chopper' Harris and Norman 'bite your legs' Hunter say it all. There was however another side to the game – the mavericks. George Best is the best known of these outlaws on the pitch who refused to relinquish skill for hard work; the others include Tony Currie, Alan Hudson, Rodney Marsh and Frank Worthington. What united them was not simply how they played on the field: for them flair was a way of life rather than just a match-winning tactic.

Hence when his team-mates were tucked up with a mug of cocoa the night before the big game, Frank Worthington could be found strutting his stuff at the local nightclub, downing a few beers and chasing a bevy of gorgeous women. With his long hair, flamboyant clothes and taste for tacky jewellery, he was a rebel and proud of it.

He tells all in his autobiography, appropriately named, *One Hump or Two*, a book that reads like a shopping list of his sexual conquests. Miss Barbados, Lindy Field, at least two Miss Great Britains, Mandy Rice-Davies, Jilly Johnson, married women, single women, young women, older women – no one it seems could resist his charm.

No wonder his first wife Birgitta, a Swedish model, cited his infidelity when she divorced him. And no wonder his second wife of 10 years, Carol, a former page three girl, is used to the sympathetic looks that say he must be cheating on her but she's too in love with him to admit it.

Carol is no dim-witted victim, she's a fighter. Fiercely proud of her husband, she lives with his reputation but demands respect in return. 'Whenever Frank is referred to in the papers, it's always womanizing, playboy Frank Worthington. I find that really insulting. It assumes he hasn't changed, but also, that I would be willing to put up with him running around. It's disrespectful to me.'

Carol Worthington is a woman who knows her own mind. No wonder her husband describes her as a 'cross between Kim Basinger, a Tasmanian devil with a touch of Eva Braun'. She also knows the football world inside out: her father was Noel Dwyer, a former West Ham and Wolves goalkeeper, and someone, she says, 'who had a bit of a reputation' himself. So she is unequivocal about what sort of behaviour she expects from Frank, and it doesn't include nights out with the lads. 'I know what they get up to when they're all together,' she says. 'They behave like drunken sex maniacs. I've told Frank, if he starts gallivanting, I'm off, it's as simple as that.'

Page three girls are not generally perceived as strong women, rather the opposite: glamorous airheads, dollybirds without two brain cells to rub together. They are, some feminists imply, pathetic creatures who can't see that their trade – soft porn – makes them mere sex objects. Carol, according to this analysis, would be quite content to be the sexual object on the arm of some successful man.

Carol laughs at the very idea. 'When I met Frank, I was as successful as him. I had just as many people recognizing me in the street as he did,' she says. 'As for being a gold-digger, I made

**113**

my own living and a good one – I lived in a penthouse flat opposite Harrods.'

Her view was that she knew exactly what she was doing. She wasn't trying to overturn years of patriarchy, but she was no push-over either. As Madonna, the Spice Girls and numerous other powerfully sexy women have shown, being glamorous doesn't mean you are not in control.

'I was never willing to let men walk all over me,' Carol says. 'Quite the opposite, when I started seeing Frank, it was on my terms.' They met in a nightclub in Birmingham in 1979, just after Frank had signed for Birmingham City. Her first impression was not favourable. He was weighed down with gold jewellery: two medallions round his neck, a dress watch, a bracelet and three rings, and he was wearing leather trousers, in short an out and out fashion disaster.

But he was obviously smitten with her. 'He used to follow me around like a little boy,' she explains. 'When I left one nightclub to go on to a bar, five minutes later in he would trot. I loved it.' Carol's friends warned her against getting involved. Her mother was ready to whack Frank with a broom should he ever dare to set foot across her threshold. 'A leopard never changes its spots,' she told her daughter.

They needn't have worried. 'I wouldn't let him come near me,' Carol says. 'I wasn't going to be another notch on his bedpost. But I think that was part of my attraction, the more I ignored him the more he chased me.'

**114**

Even when they did start 'seeing each other', it was not serious. 'Well not on my part, anyway,' she says. 'I was 21 when we met, far too young to settle down, so I just saw him when it suited me.'

This is not the story that Frank Worthington would like his public to know. 'He cherishes and protects his image,' Carol says. 'He wants people to think he's irresistible to women.' But if the need arises, Carol is quick to put him in his place. 'As soon as he starts to crane his neck to get an eyeful of some attractive woman who's just walked in a room, I tell him: "I don't know what they see in you at your age," or that he's a dirty old man, a letch.'

Vivacious and charming, Carol now acts as her husband's agent in her own inimitable style. The background role is not for her. I first met Carol at a cabaret evening in London where Frank was due to perform his act – reminiscences of his days as a player combined with renditions of his hero Elvis Presley's most famous songs. The first words I heard her speak regarded accommodation: 'You've put us in a hotel full of drug dealers,' she said of the two star hotel in the middle of King's Cross, 'we can't stay there. So I've booked us into a four star hotel, and I'm sending you the bill,' she told the harassed organizer. Typical of the footballer who is used to having everything arranged for him, Frank stood silently by.

When Frank came on stage, Carol was determined the evening was going to be a success. 'This is the first time he's sung in public, so I want it to go well for him,' she said. Having the evening going well meant, Carol decided, that all the audience had to dance along to his songs.

When the first strains of 'All Shook Up' came over the speakers, she shouted to the 200-strong audience: 'Come on you lot!' They seemed unwilling to dance. Unperturbed, Carol put her glass of white wine to one side, threw her Chanel jacket to the floor and strode over to the front of the stage pulling a couple of startled members of the audience with her as she went. She then proceeded to engage them in a slow cancan. Tottering on her high heels, bleached blonde hair flashing from side to side, she galvanized the audience – they didn't know whether to look at Frank or Carol. Her husband's bemused look was that of someone who has seen it all before.

'Come on, let's get some atmosphere going,' she shouted. She certainly did that: by the end of Frank's second song the entire audience was moving in time to the music.

After he had finished his performance, Carol declared the evening a success. 'Thank God I don't have to do that every night,' she said. In fact, contrary to popular opinion, they now lead a quiet life. Most nights they are snuggled up in bed by eight o'clock watching the early evening film.

'People say Frank's much quieter when I'm around,' Carol says, 'so I suppose I've tamed him to a certain extent.' Under Carol's influence, they now enjoy quiet meals out rather than late nights nightclubbing: 'Neither of us want to do that anymore.'

But there are still remnants of the old Frank. Carol maintains that her husband is still vain: 'Every time we pass a shop window, he'll

**116**

be trying to get a glimpse of his reflection.' And he still has an eye for the women. 'Can you believe it,' Carol says with her slight Birmingham accent, 'his favourite TV programme isn't football, it's *Fashion TV*, particularly when the models are parading around in their underwear.'

But Frank has very little time to indulge his roving eye. Carol is the one who organizes his diary, so she knows where he is 'all the time'. And when he goes away on football tours – he plays for Emlyn Hughes' All Star charity football team – Carol insists on going too.

It is perhaps fortunate that Carol met Frank at the end of his playing career, when he was no longer expected to go on club tours. For it is quite conceivable that Carol would have demanded that the manager explain why wives couldn't go too. Even in the All Star team, wives have to make their own way, and are expected to stay in a different hotel. 'It's so old-fashioned,' she said. 'On Frank's last tour, I had to sneak up the fire escape in order to sleep with my husband.'

Frank Worthington was one of the first footballers to perceive himself as an entertainer as well as a sportsman, and to want to mix with other entertainers. As Carol says: 'Both Frank and I wanted to have a good time – for a while that is what we had in common.' They met because they both enjoyed nightclubs, bands and late nights – certainly not because Carol wanted to hook a footballer.

In fact, Frank had much to gain from their liaison, in so much as it did wonders for his much cherished reputation. That was part of the reason he pursued Carol so ruthlessly and finally won her

**117**

over. Having Carol as his wife maintains Frank's image as the man who can have in the flesh what so many men can only look at in the newspapers.

Carol acknowledges there is a grain of truth in that. 'I remember going to watch him play at Birmingham City, when I was at the height of my fame. And crowds of lads were singing: "Get your tits out for the lads." I was so embarrassed. But Frank, he was in his element. I could see him preening. He liked the idea that his girlfriend was someone the other lads could only dream about.'

## Phyllis Liddell and Jess Paisley

There is no greater symbol of the golden age of football than Liverpool Football Club. Noted for its free-flowing style of play, wealth of talented players and managers, and for scooping up more major national and international honours than any other team, Liverpool has had a whole series of golden ages.

One of Liverpool's greatest players – some say the greatest of all time – was Billy Liddell. Nicknamed 'the flying Scot', he played for the club during the Second World War and throughout the 1950s. While this is not considered one of the club's greatest eras, Billy Liddell, a talented winger cum centre forward, single-handedly maintained Liverpool as a force to be reckoned with. The club's legions of loyal supporters renamed Liverpool as 'Liddellpool' in his honour.

Looking back, it is strange to imagine that Billy was equivalent in stature to the likes of Robbie Fowler and Steve McManaman today. Their lives are certainly very different. While Steve and Robbie drive top of the range BMWs, own plush apartments on Liverpool's trendy Albert Dock and are mobbed by gangs of teenage girls whenever they are out in the city, Billy's circumstances were rather more modest.

Billy and his wife Phyllis, both in their 70s, live in a semi-detached house just beyond the city centre. Billy played in the days before the maximum wage was abolished in 1966, and hence the very most he earned was £20 a week. 'But,' Phyllis says: 'it was a good wage in those days, more than a skilled worker earned.' Yet it was not the only job he had; throughout his playing career he carried on working as an accountant for a local firm.

That was where he met Phyllis. 'Bill's parents refused to let him move down from Scotland and sign for Liverpool unless he had a job. They wanted him to have a career other than football because it is such a short life.'

What this did mean was that Billy was not perceived by his family as a big-shot footballer. Their children used to say to their friends, almost as an afterthought: 'Oh, he also plays football.' Phyllis followed her husband home and away – away games meant making her own way as the club did not provide transport for players' wives.

'My mother always said: "Whatever your husband does, you do. Wherever he goes, you go." Football came first and you came second. You accepted that.' In order to watch her husband play,

Phyllis had to find friends who would mind the children for her. Clubs didn't have crêches for players' children in those days – most still haven't – 'and you would put your children in a situation where they might be a nuisance to other people, so taking them along to games was out of the question.'

It's a situation that continues to this day. In Sue Mott's book *A Girl's Guide to Ball Games*, Shelley Webb, wife of Neil Webb, formerly of Manchester United, recalls how she was told by Alex Ferguson that the club didn't have room for a crêche for players' children. She eventually got permission to organize one herself. When her husband moved from the club, Alex Ferguson apparently said to Bryan Robson: 'Oh, so we don't need to have the crêche anymore.'

For years, Liverpool football club didn't have any facilities for players' wives. When Phyllis and Bob were first married there was not even a ladies' room. 'After the game we used to sit outside on a bench in the entrance hall underneath a plaque commemorating past club presidents,' Phyllis says. Eventually the players asked if their wives could have facilities, 'so the club put us in a little room under the stand and gave us tea and biscuits, that was it'.

What Phyllis dreaded most was seeing her husband injured. Back in the 40s and 50s, far less was known about the treatment of sporting injuries, and trained physiotherapists were few and far between. Phyllis recalls that one player lost a leg when soil got into an open wound.

'Whenever Billy went down, fear would go right through me. Once Billy and another player clashed heads, blood was streaming down their faces. Billy fell to the floor and the trainer put a towel over his head. I was in the stands with my mother, and she started to panic: "He's dead, he's dead," she cried.' Thankfully it looked worse than it was and Billy continued the game. 'But if he had been seriously injured, I wouldn't have been able to find out what was wrong. You couldn't rush down and see your husband. You were just a player's wife in those days – a non-entity.'

There was a glamorous side. Billy was invited to parties and dinners and Phyllis always went with him. They regularly travelled down to London for functions and were good friends with Frankie Vaughan and the Liverpool pools magnate, Sir John Moores. She admires Billy because he refused to attend events that she was not also invited to – many sporting evenings in those days were men only.

To begin with it was a daunting prospect. Dinner dances were inevitably formal black tie and evening dress affairs. 'I wasn't born into that sort of lifestyle and I was very shy. Players are used to having people looking at them, but I wasn't. It is frightening crossing a room and feeling hundreds of pairs of eyes on you.'

Even on these occasions, wives inevitably took a back seat. Either people would be very frightened to approach Billy and Phyllis because he was a well-known figure. They would get the sideways glances, the hushed voices as people said: 'Do you know who that is?' which Phyllis says 'could make you feel very lonely'. Or the opposite would happen: people would crowd round Billy desperate for autographs

**121**

and a chat, leaving Phyllis out in the cold. 'A man once came up to me and said: "Do you know you've been sitting on your own for half an hour? Come and join our table." People can just take over.'

Phyllis has seen enough of the intrusion into your personal life that fame brings – including having the National Express Coach slow down outside her house twice a day so the passengers could see where Billy Liddell lived – not to envy the lifestyle of players today. She would get the occasional phone call from a strange woman asking for Billy, saying he had agreed to go out with her. 'It didn't bother me,' she says. 'I trusted Billy. Well, you had to.' But it was nothing like the sort of attention players get today. 'They're superstars, aren't they? I wouldn't like not to be able to walk to the shops without everyone looking at you, having no private life.' She shook her head. 'We were happy with our lot. At the end of the day you can only wear one pair of shoes at a time, only live in one house.'

What she remembers with most affection is the genuine closeness between players' wives. 'There was no jealousy, I bet you don't get that today.' And she likes the community spirit that existed when they lived in a club house – Jess Paisley lived opposite, Phil Taylor down the road. 'We were in and out of one another's houses, and we'd all travel back together on the tram after the game. It was marvellous.'

Jess Paisley misses being part of a community too. When she opened the door of her large bungalow in a prosperous Liverpool suburb, she looked out onto the leafy crescent that was devoid of noise or people. 'I preferred living in our old semi,' she says. 'Then you knew your neighbours. Here you hardly see anyone at all.'

Jess moved to her current home because her husband Bob hated fuss. He wanted to live somewhere secluded so that on the rare occasions he did spend time at home, he wouldn't be bothered by fans. There were plenty of those in Liverpool during the 1970s because Bob became a legend in his own lifetime.

He was one of the greatest managers of all time, in the same league as Sir Matt Busby, Jock Stein and his predecessor Bill Shankly. During his nine years as manager of Liverpool FC, the team won 13 trophies: three European cups, six league championships, three league cups and one UEFA cup. Only Alex Ferguson has since come anywhere near emulating his achievements.

Despite their good fortune, Jess continues to live modestly. Hers is not an ostentatious house. There is no mock Tudor frontage, or a swimming pool at the back – although she does have a large, well kept garden – and there are no gargantuan sofas sagging beneath the weight of stuffed satin cushions. Her sitting room is comfortable and homely, sporting chintz curtains, a fireplace adorned with porcelain trinkets and a three-piece suite that she has no doubt had for a good few years but can't see the point in replacing when it's perfectly serviceable.

**123**

Like her home, Jess Paisley has no airs or graces. Small and slightly chubby, she has a keen sense of humour; the only time she ceases to smile is when she talks about her late husband. He died in her arms in February 1996, just two months before I spoke to her, and she admitted her life felt empty without him. Her sentences invariably began with 'Bob liked… ' or 'Bob would be sitting over there,' she would point wistfully to the empty chair, 'and he'd say… '

The terrible irony is that after years of hard work, Bob and Jess were looking forward to spending their retirement together when Bob started to exhibit the first signs of Alzheimer's disease. She remembers that time well. 'He was driving the car not far from where we live, and he suddenly said: "Which way do I go?" I told him not to be soft, I thought he was joking, but he wasn't.'

Alzheimer's causes a progressive decline in the ability to remember, learn or think. The loss of short-term memory is an early sign. Disorientation, confusion with time and place and wandering are symptoms. As the disease progresses, the loss of the ability to think becomes more and more marked. Simple tasks like tying shoe-laces or telling the time become impossible. It inevitably puts the families of people who suffer under enormous strain.

The disease is common among footballers, and one line of reasoning suggests that the heading of a football over the years, especially the heavy leather balls used during the 40s and 50s, can be a contributory factor. Danny Blanchflower and Joe Mercer both died of Alzheimer's.

**124**

Jess has every reason to feel bitter: the game that was her husband's life ultimately killed him. But she isn't. She is gut-wrenchingly sad: 'The times we could have enjoyed together we couldn't... ' she tails off. 'We didn't know there was a link in those days, so we couldn't have done anything about it. And anyway, I wanted Bob to be happy and for him that meant playing football.' End of story.

Indeed she takes great pride in her husband's achievements. While the house is certainly not a shrine to him, his presence is everywhere. There are more silver platters, cups and caskets discretely displayed against the pretty floral wallpaper than many a club can boast in its whole history. I asked about a large conical-shaped object high up on top of a cabinet. 'That was what Bob won when he was made manager of the year for the third time,' Jess said casually. 'The other five (he received the award an incredible six times) are at the club – I can't get everything in the house.'

You get the impression that she would have been no less proud of her husband if he had not decided to pursue a career in football management but reverted to his trade as a bricklayer. For Jess simply adored the man she met one fateful day in 1945 'on the midnight train to London'. He was a soldier stationed in London who travelled north at weekends to play for Liverpool FC and she was a teacher from Liverpool going on holiday to London. Jess had never heard of Bob Paisley. 'He was just the man who threw his coat on my sandwiches,' she says.

Bob could not have achieved cabinets full of cups without the support Jess gave him. When Bob hung up his boots in 1953, he did not enjoy the financial security that players do today. Finishing playing was a precarious time for a footballer. There were no pension schemes, many players were not educated to do anything else, and football clubs were quite ruthless in letting players go with little more than a thank you. Loyal players just had to accept that they were surplus to requirement. Tommy Lawton, the magnificent Everton and Chelsea centre forward of the 1940s, descended on such hard times when his career ended that he had to sell his cups and medals just to keep himself afloat.

When Bob finished playing, he and Jess still lived in a club house – which could be repossessed for another player at any time – and they had three young children to support. When the club offered Bob the job of second team trainer, it was a mixed blessing. True, he wanted to carry on working in football, but Jess says: 'He was offered only £10 a week – less than he earned as a player – and that wasn't much.'

Because Jess 'wanted what Bob wanted', she made it possible for him to pursue his football dreams. 'I said to Bob: "I think I'd better go back to work." He replied: "I think you better had."' She went back to teaching at the local primary school, ostensibly for a few weeks, and ended up staying 23 years, until she retired.

She now thinks it was a form of salvation, because as Bob progressed from second to first team trainer, to coach and eventually in 1974 to manager, he was increasingly absent from home. For years the only time she saw her husband was 'at breakfast time and on a Sunday afternoon, if the team weren't playing away'. Even though, as Bob

126

progressed at the club, she no longer had to work for financial reasons, having a job gave Jess her own life. 'The last thing I wanted was to be a clinging vine. Because if Bob was worrying about me, he wouldn't be doing his job properly, and I didn't want that.'

On the backs of such sacrifices are great football managers created. While Bob Paisley's honours are well documented, the role his wife played behind the scenes has gone without recognition by either the club or the press.

Like many successful men, Bob relied on his wife to take care of the running of the house and looking after the family so he could devote himself to football. But Jess stresses that neither she nor the children felt neglected: 'Bob was still playing when the children were very small, so they saw a lot of him because he was at home most afternoons.' When he became Liverpool manager, inevitably his workload increased dramatically, and the family worked around that. 'It simply made the time we had together more special,' she explains.

The demands of his job as manager did mean that on occasion he had an otherworldly sense of family affairs. He did not take on the duties that fathers traditionally do. She smiles when she recalls a time when the children were reaching adolescence. 'They were upstairs making such a racket, I said to Bob: "Listen to that." He sat there with the paper and said, in a tone that didn't even permeate the ceiling: "Be quiet, boys." I was the one who had to go up and sort it out.'

**127**

Jess had very little direct involvement in Bob's footballing career. 'That was his own business,' she says. He didn't reveal too much about the pressures of management. 'If the team lost, I'd make sure I was in bed before he came back at night, so I could just say "hello". He'd be quiet and go into his shell a bit.' But, she adds: 'You have to be patient, you have to let them sort themselves out. I did it by just being there, continuing to care for him.'

## Norah Mercer – no ordinary Joe

Like Jess Paisley, Norah Mercer was a manager's wife. But unlike Jess, she has a rather more sombre tale to tell. Norah is a charming host. The trolley laden with tea and cakes was ready when I arrived. 'Try the coffee cake,' she cajoled. 'It's homemade, not too dry, don't you think?' She likes her guests to feel comfortable: 'Are you warm enough dear?', 'Can I get you anything else?' And she takes a real interest in what you are doing – but not so much as to be pushy. If you would like to tell her, she would be very interested to hear. It's an echo, no doubt, of how she cared for her husband.

The football wives I spoke to were invariably warm characters. They are perhaps used to chivvying along their single-minded spouses, who get frustrated by injuries, irritated by defeat and frightened at the prospect of never being able to play again.

They are certainly adept at looking after their husbands. Was her husband handy around the house? I asked Norah. She didn't need to think long. 'He could boil the kettle... yes, he could make a cup

**128**

of tea. Anything more… no – he couldn't peel potatoes or boil an egg.' But then Norah wouldn't expect him too. It's each person to their trade: Joe Mercer's was football, Norah's was the house and caring for her husband. 'I never questioned that, I didn't want to be a nagging wife.'

Norah's fortitude was tested during her 49-year marriage to 'the nicest man in football'. Joe Mercer, remembered for his twinkling smile and down-to-earth comments, was a magnificent player for both Everton and Arsenal. He went on to become a successful club manager, most notably at Manchester City during the late 60s, and was even caretaker manager of the England squad.

But just as Kenny Dalglish cracked under the pressure of management, so did Joe Mercer. After two less-than-successful stints, first at Sheffield United and then at Aston Villa – both clubs were relegated – Joe had a severe stroke. To add insult to injury, Dick Wragg, the chairman of Sheffield United, sent a telegram: 'Congratulations, you've done it again!'

'That is the worst thing about football,' Norah says, 'when the crowd and the directors attack you. Because what can you do? You can only do your best.'

A year later Manchester City offered him the manager's job. 'I wanted him to pack it in,' she says. 'Of course the decision was up to him – it always was. But I felt he should put his health first.' Her husband chose to accept the position and like the tower of strength she is, Norah threw herself into supporting him.

**129**

'My son David said: "If he goes back and it kills him, that would be awful. But if you don't let him go back, he's going to die sitting in that chair." And he was right, football was Joe's lifeblood. He had to go back.'

But didn't she worry the stress might make him ill again – perhaps even kill him – which would affect not only his life but hers too? 'I'm one of those old-fashioned folks who believes a man must do what he wants.' She adds firmly: 'I'm not a feminist. You had to accept that you came second to football.'

Jess Paisley knows all about that. At Bob's funeral, even the bishop quoted a remark made in the newspapers that football was more important to Bob than his wife. 'I knew it was true,' Jess says, 'but it never bothered me. We knew the relationship we had. He always knew I was getting along quite merrily, that all I wanted was for him to do well.' It's a point Norah Mercer would back all the way.

## Ann Brightwell – gold medal mum

Ann Brightwell is a soccer mum who is famous in her own sporting right. A pair of muddy running shoes outside the door of her home, a smart townhouse in the Cheshire town of Congleton, provide a clue to her previous occupation.

Better known by her maiden name, Packer, Ann won the women's 800 metres by a phenomenal five metres at the 1964 Tokyo games, setting a world record in the process. She is one of only five British women to win an Olympic track and field event since the war.

Today she still runs 'but only to keep in shape – three times a week'. For the rest of the time she enjoys cooking, tends to her immaculate garden, and looks after her husband, the silver medallist sprinter Robbie Brightwell, and her three boys.

Ann decided to retire at the very pinnacle of her career. 'Had I been able to make a living out of sport I would have continued, but that wasn't an option.' She married Robbie – and over the next few years gave birth to three boys, all of whom inherited their parents' sporting prowess: Gary, the eldest, in junior athletics and the younger boys, Ian and David, in professional football. Both started out at Manchester City: Ian is still there, David now plays for Bradford.

'I suppose we are a sporty family. We exposed the boys to a wide range of sports: they swam, played cricket, rugby and athletics. But we never consciously thought of football. It was a bit of luck really, and as far as Ian and David are concerned, a great deal of determination.'

Ann and Robbie were careful not to force sport onto their sons – particularly athletics – for fear they would feel they had to live up to their parents' high standards. It was more a case of 'doing what all parents do and encouraging your children's interests'.

She glows with delight when she talks about her two sons. What was her proudest moment? Ian getting selected for the England

**131**

Under 21 squad is certainly up there, as was watching her 'Brightwell boys', as they were known, playing in the same City first team – Ian in midfield, David at left back. What gives her most pleasure is that Ian has developed into a sporting professional.

'Ian was a very competitive little boy. Whenever we played in the garden he would sulk if he was bowled out. If they had a race and Ian didn't win, we had to get the handicapping just right so that he could. I was worried that he wouldn't be able to control his temper, that he would get a bad name. But, to his credit, he has never reacted in a non-positive way.'

In Britain we hear about 'Worcester woman' but in the USA the emblematic woman voter is the soccer mum. Well, here is one in Britain. Like many mothers, Ann's first introduction to the game came when she ferried both sons to junior football matches – an arduous 40 mile round trip. 'It was a nightmare,' she says. 'I had no sooner got home from dropping them off than I had to get back in the car and pick them up again. I said as much to the trainer: "Well, if you want them to play in a Mickey Mouse team," was his gruff response. I hung my head in shame and continued to take them.'

'I'm pleased I did,' she adds, with a look that suggests she is glad those days are over, 'because he was the one who helped them get as far as they have.' The club was a regular haunt for Manchester City scouts. 'I realized that they would have access to all the best coaches and other opportunities if they made the grade with that guy, so you had to find a way.' She was right. Ian and David

progressed to Manchester City's schoolboy team and finally signed
professional terms.

But it was not all plain sailing from there on. It wasn't a question
of Ann and Robbie turning up at games and congratulating themselves on their son's good fortunes. As parents concerned for their
children, they had all the emotional traumas that come with high
level sport to contend with.

'It must be difficult for parents who don't come from a sporting
background,' Ann admits, 'because sometimes children can upset
their parents. Sport has a lot of nasty sides, emotionally draining
sides: injuries, being dropped. I suppose we were better able to
deal with that because we were on the same wavelength. We
understand that the worst thing for a sportsman is not to be able
to do the thing he loves. We knew when to stand back and not
to talk about it, and when to say something.'

Even so, Ann found some of the club's methods perplexing. 'The
manager obviously has a very difficult job bringing out the best
from very different players, but I do think that sometimes the
man-management is not as good as it could be.' A player, for
example, may find out he has been dropped via a note on the
notice board, with no explanation offered. 'That may make some
players more hungry, more determined to do better. Others may
not react very readily to being told: "You're rubbish, go and play
in the reserves until you are good enough," or not being told
anything at all.

**133**

'As a parent I know that my sons have different personalities, they respond differently to criticism. Ian may not be the best player on the pitch, but he works hard, he will run all over, give 100 per cent. David, on the other hand, is more hesitant, a careful player, he'll take the trouble to make sure the ball doesn't go offside.' Ann favours a softer management style: 'I don't think it detracts from anyone's authority to say: "In my opinion you are not playing as well as you were last week, I'd like to give you a rest."'

Ann was never a football fan until the boys started playing. 'We go to watch the lads, I can't say we'd go every week otherwise.' These days, with the boys at different clubs, she and Robbie either have to split up – taking one game each – or alternate between the clubs. But she does enjoy it: 'I like the fact that there's no snobbery at football, you're all just fans.'

The Brightwell home is certainly not a shrine to the athletic talents of its occupants. Ann's Olympic gold medal isn't even on display: 'It was all a long time ago,' she says simply. No reason then for the boys to feel in their shadow? 'None at all. They didn't live through the short period when people were fascinated by us.' For a time the fairytale romance between Ann and Robbie – two of Britain's finest athletes – captured the heart of the nation. The look of unbridled joy on Ann's face as she ran straight into the arms of Robbie – then her fiancé – after crossing the 800 metres winning line, is a defining image of the Tokyo games. Indeed it was that self-same smile that inspired film-maker David Putnam to produce the award-winning *Chariots of Fire*. But once Ann and Robbie married and retired from athletics, that intense interest died down. 'By the time the boys became aware of what we did, no one was talking about it anymore,' she says.

That doesn't stop people assuming that their children got where they are because of their parents, 'that all we had to do was phone Manchester City and they were in,' Ann laughs. 'It is unfair because anyone involved in football knows how tough it is. If you don't make the grade you are out.' Even the Manchester City programme regularly referred to the Brightwell boys as son of… 'They laugh about it now, but they went through a phase of thinking: "Why do they always say that?" After a certain stage they have a right to be judged on their own merits.'

Thirty-three years after her Olympic victory, Ann Brightwell doesn't have time to dwell on those days. The phone rang frequently during the interview, evidence of a vibrant social life. Then there are the 'boys' to think of. They have benefited from the way sport has changed since the 1960s. Both are able to do what their mother could not – make a good living out of their chosen field. Ann Brightwell could not be more pleased.

## Gayle Blanchflower – not just the glory days

Gayle Blanchflower lives under a shadow. An extremely successful business woman – she's a freelance advertising executive – she owns a smart flat in posh Maida Vale, and her name can be found on the guest list of many a celebrity party. But whenever people hear her name, they inevitably say: 'Any relation to Danny?'

'I never ask people their surnames,' she says, because she knows the conversation will ultimately lead to her father. Danny Blanchflower, with his hair slicked back, shiny with pomade, looks like a 1950s matinée idol in his photos. He was one of the most intelligent players the game has produced: skilful, tactical and a born leader. To many fans he is one of the game's true statesmen. To his daughter he was 'a father who was never there'.

People can't hear enough about Danny Blanchflower, the captain of Spurs when they won the 1960–61 League and FA Cup double. They want to hear about Danny the footballer, they don't want to know what he was really like.

In truth, many think they do know. An image of the Blanchflower family is etched in our popular memory. Danny was one of the first footballers to appear in a television advert – for Shredded Wheat. In 1958, thousands of people saw the family sitting round their breakfast table: Danny, the solid hard-working footballer with his adoring family. Gayle was there. She was the one to whom he uttered those famous words that became a catchphrase across the breakfast tables of Britain: 'Pass the hot milk please.'

People don't want to know the Danny that existed off the field, or off the television set, so Gayle would rather not talk about her father. 'I wish I'd changed my name when I left Southgate (the north London suburb in which she grew up), then I'd be free of him.' She doesn't want to lie. But when she's asked about him, people get angry about what they hear. Not with Danny – with Gayle.

'I have told people what sort of father he was in the past and it backfires against me. People say: "You shouldn't say things like that." He was their hero. I'm bursting bubbles. I am proud of his achievements but not of him as a man and certainly not as a father.'

In one sense there is not very much to tell. Danny was one of football's absent fathers. 'I didn't know what it was like to have a normal father who was home every evening. I knew he was different – successful even – but it didn't impress us. We used to use his trophies as doorstops.' Danny was a reluctant father: what free time he did have he used to spend on the golf course. 'He had to be forced to go on family holidays, preferring to holiday alone or with friends.'

In the minds of those around her he was the perfect father, a perplexing situation for a young girl. 'I was invited to all my schoolfriends' birthday parties because their fathers worshipped him and their mothers fancied him. They foolishly thought he would either take me to the party or come pick me up. But, of course, he did neither.'

Gayle was also very popular with boys. At school dances there were always plenty of admirers asking to walk her home. 'It would be: "Can I come in then?" I knew from my friends that the guys usually just wanted to bugger off, they knew their parents would be in. I would say: "He's not here." "OK, bye then." I'd be left watching them walk away. Pathetic.' No wonder football miraculously doesn't seem to work on her TV set.

Danny Blanchflower is renowned for his serious, dedicated approach to football and life, but Gayle sees him somewhat differently. 'He was a solitary and uncommunicative father. You either had to talk about football or he had nothing to say.' Danny thought that her job in advertising was 'a load of rubbish', and she hates football, 'so we didn't have much to talk about'. It must upset her but she doesn't let it show. 'I've never known any different, so I don't have a comparison.'

Danny's private life was a mess. Gayle's mother, his second wife, threw him out after discovering he was having a child with another woman only six months after she had given birth to Gayle's younger sister. While they were married, there was constant friction because of his jealous and resentful nature.

'He feared my mother might upstage him. She is very glamorous, the life and soul of the party. She loved going out to receptions, having a drink and meeting people. He didn't drink and he had nothing to say, so he used to get jealous. He was always trying to get her to leave.'

Gayle even thinks he resented her. She hadn't seen him in six years when she 'happened to be passing' Chelsea FC one Saturday afternoon. 'I thought I'd go in for a free post-match drink. The reception wasn't welcoming. "What are you doing here? You should phone first." Any other father would be pleased to see his daughter, but I was stealing his thunder. It took the emphasis away from him – people might take an interest in me. He said: "If you want to come again, you can go in the back room and dish out the tea to the old age pensioners." With that he walked over to the other side of the room. I didn't bother again.'

Prior to that they had pretty much lost touch anyway. 'When I left home I tried to keep in contact with him. I phoned him every month and each time he would say: "We must get together, what's your phone number?" I thought: "How many times do I have to tell you?" So I gave up.'

Ironically, she thinks she and her family (her mother, brother and sister) fared far better than his third family. 'At least my mother was stable.' Danny's third wife would think nothing of leaving their two adolescent children while she went back and forth to South Africa. 'And he would think nothing of going on a golfing trip for a week. So those kids, at 12 and 14, were left to run riot by both parents.'

Her step-sisters, she says, 'are bitter and twisted. Both are out of work and have got no sense of direction. They've made more of being Danny Blanchflower's kids because it's all they have to hang on to. But they didn't live during those great "glory, glory years" of the early 60s.'

Gayle remembers the time well. She attended that 1961 FA Cup final. 'My parents had separated and he couldn't take along his latest mistress, so I went.' She didn't enjoy the match: 'It was in the days of those old wooden rattles and there were all these men cursing and cheering.' But the banquet at the Savoy was more exciting.

'I didn't see my father at all. Dave Mackay's wife Isobel looked after me. And when we went into the reception I saw Dickie Henderson who used to compare *Saturday Night at the London Palladium*. I was

139

so gobsmacked. Everyone else was saying: "Look, Spurs are here."
I was impressed by Dickie Henderson.'

Four years after her father's death in 1993, Gail is still trying to put
those 'glory, glory days' behind her. Her family are in conflict with
her step-sisters over his estate. 'It will be a relief to get it out of the
way,' she admits. Maybe then she can lay that shadow to rest. She
knows there will always be questions, but at least her association
with him will finally be ended. She can close that chapter in her life.

'I've got my own life to lead,' she says, and with a wry smile adds,
'Do you know, it's a damn sight more interesting than his.'

one of the lads

# Behind the Ball

## Giving the Game a Feminine Touch

### Pat Smith, Deputy Chief Executive of the FA

Pat Smith's office in Lancaster Gate is that of someone who is ruthlessly efficient: there are no stray papers strewn across her desk, no dirty coffee cups littering the horizon. Dressed in a smart shirt and skirt, Pat Smith exudes confidence and serenity. At 51 years of age she has one of the top jobs in football, deputy chief executive of the Football Association. Only Graham Kelly is her senior.

Don't run away with the idea that we are talking about a zone of liberation here; football has always been run by men, and broadly, it still is. But slowly we are witnessing the hard-won benefits of those women who have painstakingly fought their way into senior jobs in football. There are not many, but in the late 1990s there are more than ever before.

Pat admits it has not been easy. Her route to the top has been gradual; she has kept her head down not only taking on any task placed in front of her, but putting in hours of work to make sure it is done to the best of her ability. Despite her high position at the FA, Pat remains relatively unknown outside the organization's Lancaster

Gate offices. Not that Pat is troubled by this. 'I tend to adopt a low profile. If I wanted a higher profile I could have it but that takes time, it means that you are not getting on with your day job and my job involves an awful lot of paperwork.' You can see why when she reels off her diverse list of responsibilities: director of ticketing, pricing and protocol for major tournaments like Euro 96, stand-in for Graham Kelly at meetings and events, as well as being the hub of the office, the point of contact for all the FA's different departments.

Pat never set out to get this far. But she is ambitious, a self-confirmed workaholic who has seized every opportunity to develop her areas of responsibility because 'I like to get as much out of a job as I possibly can'. It is a far cry from the days when she first joined the FA as a secretary after leaving school. Having been an Enfield Town supporter since she was a child, working for the FA was her dream job.

The FA tended to be run according to a culture of amateurism which meant that people – invariably men – were employed because of their knowledge and interest in sport, rather than because they had business or administration skills. It was possible for their secretaries – invariably women – to become closely involved in the day-to-day running of the organization – even if they didn't get the credit for it – because they could provide that organizational backbone. Many, single-handedly, kept their bosses' affairs in order and the departments they headed running smoothly.

In 1977, Pat became PA to the then head of the FA Ted Croker. 'To make our business successful, an awful lot of strong administration and teamwork is needed. So I took on a lot more responsibilities as the years went by with Ted Croker, so much so that I did feel aggrieved when people perceived me as a glorified secretary. I was doing what I considered to be even more than a head of department's job. I was shadowing him and keeping everything ticking over. He was a very charismatic figure, his skill was going out and selling the FA as opposed to being a desk person. So I tended to stay at Lancaster Gate and keep the day-to-day things running.'

So important was Pat to the running of Ted Croker's department that when he became ill, Pat essentially stood in for him. When Graham Kelly became the new chief executive in 1989 she was determined that she would not continue with the title of PA because that was simply not the job she was doing. After a stint as the administration manager she became the deputy chief executive – a new position created especially for her. But Pat's story highlights the fate of many women: it is assumed that they will be content to go back to their former role once a new permanent member of staff is in place. When Graham Kelly was appointed chief executive, one of Pat Smith's senior colleagues said: 'I assume you'll go to another secretarial job now?' 'That was someone who knew the job I was doing but couldn't accept it. If I were a man he would never have said that.'

143

Over the past few years, new opportunities for women have opened up in the running of football clubs. Once businessmen sat on football club boards for reasons of status and prestige rather than profit. Today a new breed of businessmen have come into the game, aware that they can use their acumen to run football clubs more profitably. Clubs like Manchester United and Tottenham Hotspur have become public limited companies with annual turnovers of hundreds of millions of pounds. Treating a football club as a business means professionalizing its operation, placing increasing emphasis on marketing, corporate sponsorship and merchandising. Women with commercial experience have found employment in these developing areas. Some clubs have been bought by wealthy businessmen as another facet of an already substantial business empire. Birmingham City was bought by David Sullivan, owner of the *Daily* and *Sunday Sport*, Blackpool was bought by property tycoon Owen Oyston. In both cases these men have installed female managing directors from other branches of their empires, to run the business end of their newly-found footballing interests: Karren Brady at Birmingham and Gill Bridge at Blackpool.

## Karren Brady – the lady stings the blues

Karren Brady's appointment in 1993 raised many an eyebrow within the footballing establishment. At just 23 years of age she was deemed little more than a PR stunt, the product of one of David Sullivan's flamboyant attempts to get publicity for his club. Despite an impressive track record in advertising and marketing with Saatchi and Saatchi, LBC and the *Daily Sport*, the undeniably talented Brady has had to fight to be taken seriously. 'People who see successful women think there must be an angle there. It's too good to be true to that a woman from a good upbringing can walk into a job and be a director. They think: "Oh well, she's bonking the boss,"' Brady said in an interview with *GQ* magazine.

Indeed she is still far better known for marrying former Birmingham City centre forward Paul Peshisolido than for the fact that under her the club has, for the first time in its history, made a trading profit. 'It's not like I said: "There's a whole team to pick from. Who shall I sleep with?" The majority of people do meet their partners in the work place,' Karren said when the tabloids couldn't believe their good luck: here was a woman doing exactly what it was expected any female connected with a football club would do – bringing sex into the equation.

What Karren Brady has really brought to Birmingham City is a fresh approach. With a commercial rather than a footballing background, she was able to look at the organization of Birmingham City in the cold light of day. As an outsider, she wasn't blinkered by an affection for football's glorious – and in some cases mythical – past, that has made many senior managers resilient to change. She was therefore prepared to make far-reaching changes in the interests of doing her job: achieving maximum profitability.

She was shocked at how Birmingham was run. In an interview in *Loaded*, she admitted: 'We had the only catering department in the world that was actually losing money. I think there's only one employee left from when I arrived. Sacking people is never nice but you can't carry people for ever.' To get gate receipts up she set up a ticket office, a junior Blues club, a supporters' club, a social club and an away travel club, as well as cut price tickets for children.

Karren Brady is a strong modern career woman. She prides herself on the long hours she puts in and her tough business style. 'I feel I've been cheated by not being born a bloke. I am probably more male than most men,' she told one newspaper in 1995. Strong words which might give the impression she has no sympathy with those who bemoan women's lack of equality in the workplace. But Brady knows she has had to work harder than the average man just to get the same respect. If she doesn't moan about that – she likes being a pioneer – she is certainly under no illusions that there are advantages and disadvantages of being a woman in a man's world. She said in the *Observer* magazine: 'There are women out there who do a million more things than I'll ever do for anybody, jobs for charities and underprivileged children, and they're not credited because that's what women do. Because I'm a woman in a man's world I get much more noted and credited for what I do. In some ways that's sad, because it shows that it's all crap about women being treated equally, and on the other hand someone has to start the ball rolling. I have a sense of saying: "Well, if I can do this then other women can too."'

## Gill Bridge – Blackpool rocked

Although she was a Liverpool supporter as a child, Gill Bridge never intended to work in football. She started working for the Owen Oyston group of companies as PA to the chairman. After working her way up through the company, she found herself overseeing the office of Second Division Blackpool when the previous managing director left suddenly. She did the job so well, she was taken on full-time three months later. At 30 years of age this former model is responsible for the club's £50 million relocation to a 200 acre site on the outskirts of town.

She admits that there was some suspicion when she was first appointed but says: 'You just have to ignore it.' Women in high profile positions are often uncomfortably visible. They stand out and have the feeling that they are constantly being watched and judged. 'It would be easy to walk around with a big chip on my shoulder,' Gill explains, 'but what's the point? That's the thing men would most like to see, then they can say you are over-reacting, you are over-sensitive. It is what happens when you enter environments where managers and chairmen are not used to working with women.'

This problem was worse for Gill and Karren because they are so young. 'There are always cynics, and being female and under 30 when I first started my job, you are bound to get critics. I got this job because of the way I worked in this business. I could not have survived – particularly as a woman – for two years if I didn't know what I was doing. I'm certainly not employed out of charity.'

Try telling that to some of football's – invariably male – 'old school'. Shortly after she became Blackpool's managing director, she was collared by one of the directors who wanted to know what she was doing at the club, after all, what on earth did she know about football? Gill said nothing: 'I bit my lip until it almost bled.' But she knows her own worth, she is confident that having business experience is far more important to her job than understanding the intricacies of the game. She explains her position thus: 'There is an idea that you need to know about four-four-two formations, wingers and leftbacks – you don't. I didn't know much about football when I started, but you learn as you go along. I don't need to know which team to put out, that's the manager's job. I need to know about the business of football, how the industry operates. And that comes with business experience; it's not the result of being able to pass a ball accurately across the pitch.'

When women do enter predominantly male spheres, there are usually preconceptions about how women behave. Some men may be hostile or patronizing, assuming that a woman knows nothing about the industry. But as Gill Bridge knows, this can have advantages. Gill is responsible for negotiating transfer deals and says that some managers let more slip than they should do, simply because they assume she knows nothing about football. 'One manager admitted to me that a player was injury-prone. In a later conversation when we came to discussing prices, he started singing the player's praises. I said: "But he can't be that good. You said he was injury-prone." You can fox around with them in that way.' They don't assume that women are as methodical or as organized as they often are.

And, of course, for the female club secretary or managing director there is the usual assumption that they are either a director's or manager's wife. On one visit to Chesterfield, Gill Bridge's husband Gary was directed to the boardroom while she was automatically led to the ladies room. She said: 'The boardroom list had G. Bridge on it, and they automatically assumed Gary was the director and I was the dutiful little wife.' But she soon put them straight: 'I told them I was the director, but my husband was quite happy to go in with the ladies if they wanted him to.'

## Alison Vaughan – the woman at Man City

Alison Vaughan was the first woman to work for Manchester City's football in the community scheme. Many of these schemes have strong links with the Professional Footballers Association and they tend to be staffed by ex-professional footballers. With the emphasis on coaching in schools, this sort of work is an obvious form of employment for players who have finished their careers. It was the first time some of them had worked with a woman.

'When I first started, some men at the club were a bit wary, they didn't know what to expect from a woman. It's a question of proving yourself.' But once they realized she had some good ideas that were of benefit to the club, 'they were just brilliant – I just couldn't ask for more support,' she says. Today the chairman, managing director and team captain regularly attend events she organizes.

Alison started working at Maine Road voluntarily for a couple of months after she had finished a teacher training course. She started out showing visiting schoolchildren around the club and doing basic football coaching. Alison created her own job when she came upon the idea that football clubs could have a more direct input into the education of children in the local community. Using her teaching

149

skills, she wrote a workbook that corresponded with the primary school curriculum, based on Manchester City's footballing activities. It was the first time anyone had devised a scheme whereby children could learn through football.

She takes groups of children into the players' restaurant, where they talk about the foods players eat to keep themselves fit and healthy – a way of talking about how the body works – or they go out onto the pitch and talk about how it is cared for, how the under-soil heating works – which is a way of discussing basic science. 'The kids love it,' Alison says, 'because they don't see it as studying but as a day out at Manchester City. And when they come to open their workbooks they are very enthusiastic – which is what learning should be about.'

Alison's hard work was rewarded once the club saw that they would be able to get funding for her salary from Manchester education authority and the leisure department. As a result of her work, the club won the Littlewoods Community Award for the Premier League in 1995, and the next year Alison was voted one of *Cosmopolitan* magazine's 'Women of the Year'.

She has now broadened the scheme by inviting older children with a truancy record to come to the club for a day if they go to school for the other four. They work with Alison taking schoolchildren around the club. 'It's a real opportunity to motivate kids who just aren't interested in school. It gives them a sense of responsibility. And at the same time it's good for the club to be seen to give something back to the community.'

**150**

# Brenda Spencer – the power behind Wigan

Brenda Spencer, the chief executive at Wigan Athletic, feels that she has gained the respect of her colleagues because she has worked her way up the footballing hierarchy. An accountant by training, she reckons she has done every job in the Wigan Athletic office.

'Some women have come into football from the outside. I'm not saying they aren't good at their jobs – they are. But when it comes down to the nitty gritty, they don't know the ins and outs of running a football club, the rules and regulations of match day procedures and transfers. They will have to learn on the job and I wouldn't like that. They have to rely heavily on their club secretaries and commercial managers. It causes resentment because they think: "What does she know?" A lot of club secretaries are men who have been doing their jobs for a long time. When you have a boss telling you what to do, and they don't have the knowledge you have, it creates bad feelings. If you start at the bottom and learn slowly, it's a lot better.'

Fifty-one-year-old Brenda admits that her marriage failed because of her dedication to Wigan Athletic: 'You stop being the housewife who gets home at five o'clock and cooks the tea,' she explains. 'You end up getting back at nine or ten. It takes a special sort of fellow who can accept this – the wife phoning up and telling him she won't be home for dinner. He'll think it should be the other way round. Of course whoever's making the call is selfish but personally I don't regret any of it.'

behind the ball: giving the game a feminine touch

This is what these pioneering women needed to do in order to achieve their goals. They have had to work twice as hard as the men to get where they are. Because they have had to be so single-minded in committing themselves to their careers, they have to rule out a pleasure that many successful men enjoy, namely, a family. A man who works long hours can usually depend upon the support of his family; a woman who works long hours is liable to get divorced.

Women have made strides in getting into senior management roles in the running of professional football clubs: there are three managing directors – Gill Bridge, Karren Brady and Brenda Spencer; a growing clutch of club secretaries; and women working in the marketing departments and box offices. However, no one has crossed the rubicon to coaching or managing a professional football team. The story of Stan Hey's TV series *The Manageress*, where a female manages a second division club, still seems a distant dream.

'It's taken a hundred years to get a female managing director and it will take another hundred before we get a female manager,' Gill Bridge explains. 'Although women play a physical game, they don't play it exactly as men do. From that point of view, a woman would struggle to gain the players' respect. Football is almost like being in the army with the men out training for action. The manager has to treat them with an iron fist one minute, and the next he has to take them to one side and build up their confidence. There's a lot of psychology involved. It's also about respect. Players want to be managed by former professionals, that's who they respect. I'm respected from a business point of view. They see me in a little box: "Gill sorts out transfers but she doesn't pick the team, so that's OK." Once you try and step out of that box, it's much harder.'

No woman has tried to step out of the 'little box' Gill describes: partly because most of the women who have the experience to coach work within women's football and want to improve standards within their own sport, but also because they know that most of the jobs go to ex-professional footballers. Like Gill, most women players think a female manager or coach is, to quote Kelly Simmons, the FA's women's football coordinator, 'a long, long way off – though not impossible in the future'.

Kim Lawford, a former Southampton women's player, believes there's no inherent reason why a woman shouldn't coach a male team: 'If you can coach girls, you can coach men – the principles of implementing a playing and tactical strategy are the same.' Not that she believes it will happen for a while yet: 'I can see it would be problematic: a manager or coach needs to be in the dressing room and that could cause embarrassment and tensions among the players – the last thing you want before a big game.'

Alison Vaughan suggests that if a woman 'theoretically' did want to coach or manage a male professional team, the best way in would be for her to get her FA Advanced Coaching Licence – the highest of

**153**

the FA's four coaching awards. Not that it's an absolute pre-requisite for getting a manager's job. As Kelly Simmons says: 'There are no hard and fast rules, it's entirely down to individual clubs who they choose to manage their teams.' Some of the male managers currently working in the game who haven't played to the very highest level – although undoubtedly do have football experience – have got jobs on the strength of obtaining a coaching certificate. Kelly says: 'You don't have to be a brilliant player to be a manager or coach. Some of the best managers didn't play to the highest level but they understand tactics and how to organize a team.'

The FA's coaching courses are mixed – although the FA are organizing women-only courses to encourage more women – hence men and women learn exactly the same skills. But at the present time only two women have successfully acquired the FA Advanced Coaching Licence. Sue Lopez, a former captain of the England women's team and the Coaching and Development Officer for the Hampshire FA is one. The word is that there are more well-qualified women out there, but they are putting all their time and effort into playing: as women's football isn't professional, even its best players have to juggle work and football commitments. But once they hang up their boots, no doubt some of these women will sign up for coaching courses.

Even if they did have the FA Advanced Coaching Licence like Sue Lopez, Alison Vaughan thinks it would still be hard for a woman to break into the world of male professional football as a first team manager or coach. What's more, she thinks that given that women's football isn't professional, the time isn't right just yet: 'If you have a

154

woman up against a man with the same qualification or an ex-male professional who knows the game inside out, he would get the job. I think that's fair. It's not being sexist, it's being equal.' That is not to say it isn't worthwhile talented women players gaining coaching qualifications: the development of women's football depends upon it.

Women do coach at a lower level. Marrie Wieczorek trains both boys and girls aged up to 18 across Teesside for Middlesbrough Football Club. A former player on the England women's team, 40-year-old Marrie holds the FA coaching certificate and is currently studying for her FA Coaching Licence. Alison Vaughan coaches in primary and secondary schools throughout Manchester, as part of her football in the community brief. 'We only do a class that is mixed, boys and girls. Some children will have played for a couple of years, while there will be those who have never played before. We don't just coach the best 15 boys, but the whole class.' Alison played as a child with her brothers and has the basic skills, but would not claim to be an exceptional footballer. 'I do basic coaching, a warm-up, a running game, a basic skills session, and a small game afterwards so the kids can take that skill into a game. But at this level, an interest in football is the main thing, that's what helps you inspire enthusiasm.'

She doesn't find getting respect from the boys a problem because they are 'just so pleased' to be able to perform for a representative from Manchester City. 'And I do know a lot about football, so if the boys ask me something I can usually answer it.' What Alison does find gratifying is the girls' incredible enthusiasm: 'They are much

**155**

more eager to learn because many have never played football before. The boys don't always listen because they think they know how to do it anyway.'

## Hilda Hubert – Chopper owes it all to her

Women coaching young boys is not a new phenomenon. In the early 1950s, Hilda Hubert coached a highly successful schoolboy team in Hackney, North London. It is exactly this kind of experience that is part of football's hidden history.

When Hilda began teaching at Craven Park Junior School in 1950, being a keen sportswoman – she was a county cricket and netball player – she wanted to get involved in extra curricular sporting activities. Because few of the teachers at that school were interested in sports, she coached the girls at netball and the boys at football. 'It seemed unfair on the boys not to be able to have extra coaching,' she explains. The principle was that sporting skills can be transferred: 'Hockey has many similarities with football.'

A long-standing Spurs supporter – indeed, her father had taught her to play football as a child – she coached the boys using the push and run method developed by Spurs manager Arthur Rowe in the early 50s. To teach them how to pass the ball, the key to the push and run method, Hilda took the boys to bumpy ground not far from the school, 'where the gypsies used to tether their horses', and made them play. The boys moaned relentlessly, but their skills improved. 'It forced them to learn to pass straight to each other's

**156**

feet, otherwise the ball bounced all over,' Hilda explains. In the gym they learned how to kick a ball properly using their bare feet. 'If you didn't kick it on the top of your foot you really knew about it because it hurts,' she says.

Two seasons later, her team won the Hackney schoolboy league, much to the disgruntlement of the male coaches from some of the other schools. 'I was treated like dirt by some of those teachers,' she admits. 'They felt threatened.' To compensate for their disdain, she learned to became a formidable motivator. Her team would turn up for games to jibes from the opposing team's boys, and occasionally the teachers: 'Look at this load of sissies coached by a woman.' She had to implore her boys to ignore them. Hilda was allowed neither to be a referee nor to run the line, a standard practice for the male coaches. Those who scorned her had to eat their words when the team enjoyed a record-breaking 16 matches unbeaten. In the process she discovered two boys who went on to be well-known professional players: Ron 'Chopper' Harris, the early 70s Chelsea hard-man and captain, and his brother Alan, assistant manager at Crystal Palace, Spurs and Barcelona.

Today there are a growing number of female referees and assistant referees – the term 'linesman' has been changed as a recognition that more women are coming through. On Saturday August 31 1995, Wendy Toms became the first woman referee to take charge of a Vauxhall Conference game. Further down the ranks on the non-league circuit, referee Linda Bailey and her assistants Anne Smart and Karen Ford became the first all-female team to handle a senior men's game back in October 1995. But as yet no woman has officiated at a Premier League match. This is partly because there are so few female Class I officials (the highest of the three grades) like Wendy. As Janet Walmsley, a Class 3 referee who officiates in the Greater London League, explains: 'You really do have to start officiating in your early 20s to stand a chance of working your way up the ranks. And I think that's hard for women. Many don't even know that they can train to be referees and assistant referees – I didn't – and then they often have to take time out to have children, so that affects their progress.' And then there is the prejudice that many referees maintain right through the 'boys own culture' of football. Men such as ex-Tottenham player and TV commentator Alan Mullery just can't accept that women can do the job as well as men. Mullery made his views on female referees clear on ITV's *The Time and the Place*: 'There is a different time of the month when women have a pre-menstrual cycle … if you get a referee taking a game where there are 40,000 people … and some big hairy centre half gives her some stick at the wrong time of the month she's going to burst into tears.' As Janet says: 'There are men who think women haven't got what it takes to officiate at the highest level, but that's ridiculous. Women aren't better than men but they can be as good.'

**158**

# Janet Walmsley – woman in the middle

It is on the Sunday League circuit that women tend to cluster. Janet Walmsley was one of the first. An Arsenal supporter, she decided to become a referee when she saw an ad in the Arsenal programme back in 1979. She had gone to Arsenal with her young son because being a single parent, she was 'trying to be a man for her son because he needed a male role model'. Having seen this 'little man in black running up and down the pitch,' she thought: 'That looks interesting.'

The Football Association was amazed when Janet applied, 'but given that the Equal Opportunities Act had just been passed, they couldn't simply refuse me,' she says. 'But rather than let me loose with a roomful of male trainee referees, the FA sent a tutor round to my house. He brought a miniature football pitch and together we went through the laws of the game using little subuteo men.'

Today she gets a great deal of enjoyment out of her 'grassroots football'. She says that most teams don't give her any trouble, they are willing accept her judgement. 'Occasionally you get a player who tries to put one over you because he thinks women don't understand the laws of the game. You have to exert your authority. I tell them politely: "Excuse me, I'm in charge here, not you." I don't let them get away with anything. In most cases, if a player is going to get stroppy, he'll do it regardless of whether the referee's male or female.'

But she did get some quizzical looks from Sunday League footballers when she first started refereeing in the early 80s, and she would drive up to games on her big 250 cc motorbike, her long blonde hair streaming behind. 'They didn't know what to expect,' she laughs. 'Was I some radical feminist out to get my kicks by exerting control over men? Of course I wasn't. I am a feminist, but for me that means doing what I want to do. I'm not out to prove a point. I don't want to use football to control men.' Janet says that amongst the younger generation of men now playing in the Sunday leagues, a female referee barely warrants a second glance: 'They are far more at ease generally with women being in positions of authority.'

The most difficult aspect of officiating Sunday league football is the lack of facilities for women, Janet says. 'After a game of football you need a wash and a shower, but where can a woman get changed after the match? Certainly not in the communal changing rooms because that could be seriously misinterpreted.' Earlier this year, Janet Fewlings, a Sunday league referee in Exeter, joined the players in the showers in protest at the lack of facilities for women. She was suspended by her local FA for 'bringing the game into disrepute', only to be reinstated after she appealed. Two weeks later she was sacked, apparently because there were so many adverse remarks about her refereeing. As many female referees have noted, local FA branches are sometimes wary of female officials: 'There's always this unspoken suspicion that you are really there to meet men,' Janet Walmsley says.

# Charlotte Cowie – doctor in the dressing room

The team dressing room is still widely perceived as the ultimate male sanctum, a world most definitely purged of women. Ten years ago it would have been inconceivable that football clubs would open their firmly closed dressing room doors to a female physiotherapist or doctor. But that is slowly changing.

I met Charlotte Cowie in the medical room of Millwall Football Club, where she is the official team doctor. She is still the only female doctor working for a football league team. Wearing the official Millwall team tracksuit, she was very much at home amongst the sterile bandages and that telltale smell of liniment. One of the few medics in football who is qualified in sports science, she talked enthusiastically about her job.

Charlotte hasn't found being a woman a problem. 'If it doesn't bother you, it doesn't bother the players. But as soon as you look as if you might be embarrassed, then that's when the doubts set in. So you just have to be confident.' Having the support of the manager is crucial: 'The players take their trust from him.' But female doctors have to accept that when a new manager takes over, their days might be numbered, as not all managers approve of women working for football clubs.

Charlotte thinks there are advantages for women doctors. 'The players often feel they can be more open, they don't have to put on a big act,' she says. In a world that expects men to be tough, and never admit to having doubts and worries, a female doctor offers some players an opportunity to be more forthright in sharing their fears and vulnerabilities.

'The players know they can trust me. Football is full of gossip. If they feel the things they tell me will go further, or will affect the way they're treated by the manager, then they will clam up immediately.' No player wants to be perceived as a worrier or a nervous personality, because that might be interpreted as a weakness, a sign that they can't handle the pressure on the pitch.

Charlotte says her age – she is only 32 – has made it easier for her to build up a rapport with the players. 'They are just like boys I went to school with,' she explains. 'Perhaps women who are older would find the things that they do and the language that they use harder to handle. It doesn't bother me, and I genuinely feel that they don't sense they have to hold back in what they say. If they knew they could easily shock me, I'd be dead by now.'

While Charlotte isn't on a mission to change the way football clubs approach health and fitness, she would like to see more players taking seriously the demands football makes on their bodies. Sports science is a relatively new discipline, with its emphasis on nutrition, dietary manipulation, carbo-loading, fluid replacement and general fitness training, as well as ball play and learning skills. 'But as football becomes more physical, and the pace faster, knowing how to get the best from your body can make that one per cent difference that gets you that crucial goal,' Charlotte says. The days when players could play a game after eating a hot steak dinner, or dismiss the need for proper warm-up exercises before a match, are long gone. 'To be a

162

good footballer, you need to be a good athlete. The demands on players are completely different to what they were 10 years ago, but people are still using the same principles of coaching and care that they were before.'

Charlotte sees part of her role as trying to educate the young players – the Youth Training Scheme players – about the basic principles of sports science. It is precisely this sort of advice that players do not get from their club managers, because the principles of care and coaching that they pass on are often the ones they were taught when they were playing. Although this is beginning to change – for example, managers like Alex Ferguson and Ruud Gullit have brought nutritionists into their clubs to advise on diet – Charlotte says that in general, 'There's this "We did it this way and we won" mentality, and because the players are in awe of them, they take their views as sacrosanct.'

'The football system is very hierarchical. Players start out by cleaning other players' boots. So if you can get information to youngsters at the lowest level, then hopefully it will filter into the system in years to come. But you can't expect people from the top to take advice from anyone, they've already proved their worth.'

## Michelle Farrer – putting the sweet into FA

Few women ever get to sit on in the fabled players' dugout, or on the bench. One woman has, and she has made history doing it. At the Euro 96 games, it was easy to miss Michelle Farrer sitting in the

163

corner along with the England squad. Dressed in blue suit, her dark hair pulled back from her face and carrying a notebook and pen, Michelle is at 30 the youngest woman in a senior position at the FA, and within the organization's International Department, the first female administration manager. Working closely with Glenn Hoddle, she oversees the day-to-day arrangements of the England team: liaising with UEFA and FIFA officials, organizing hotel bookings and tickets, checking out foreign training grounds, as well as shadowing the England team throughout a tournament or game. 'I'm on hand to do anything and everything to make sure the team is as successful as possible in terms of back-up.'

When she applied for the post in 1990 there was a 'fair amount of scepticism'. Some members of the FA International Committee did not think it appropriate for a young woman to travel on official trips with a squad of 22 men. A compromise was reached: she could do the office administration, but she was most definitely not allowed to have direct involvement with the England team. 'It was only,' she explains, 'when Graham Taylor became manager that things changed. His view was that I was doing the work, so I should be given the opportunity to do the full job rather than passing on a file to someone else when it came to going on trips. He asked the FA to give me a chance.' She has never looked back since taking on the full job in 1991.

It may seem like a very glamorous occupation – staying in top class hotels, foreign travel and being on first-name terms with England's most celebrated sportsmen. But for Michelle, it's business as usual. 'I'm desperate not to make a mistake. I do think I have to be better than a man in my position. That's why I don't stop working during a trip.' While some of the other (male) staff go out window shopping or sightseeing, Michelle never does: 'It could be suggested that I'm only there for the shopping.' Neither does she use the topnotch facilities like the swimming pool and sauna that England team hotels inevitably have. 'I wouldn't want people to think I am only here to enjoy myself,' she says. Nor, perhaps, to be caught in a swimming pool, however innocent, with half the England team.

Being a woman does have its compensations. 'It is very hard for the players to say no to a woman. I'm guilty of using that at times,' she admits. 'If I want them to do something, I do ask nicely, but I know they won't bite back at me. I know that in most cases they'll do it. While I'm keen to have equal opportunities for women, at the end of the day you have to use all your skills to do the job.'

Michelle does think she has brought something different to her job that is connected to the fact that she's female. She is less interested in the coaching, in the nuts and bolts of the way players perform on the pitch than perhaps her male predecessors were, and more interested in the players themselves. 'In a sense I've made the job my own. I'm into communicating with people. The new players, for example, can phone me up and ask me what clothes they should bring when we are on tour. They wouldn't ask anybody else that. Or when they arrive they are able to ask me: "Where do we go?" They wouldn't ask a man – they'd probably pretend they knew. I try to think what they would want to know so that they are not little souls wandering around. I think they appreciate that.' As far as Michelle is concerned, the fewer worries the players have, the better she is

**165**

doing her job. Her easygoing manner, that the players do feel they can tell her their worries, for example, also begins to change the 'boys own' culture of those England team trips. She is enabling those players to behave in a slightly more open way.

She negotiates the gender difference well. She makes it clear to the players that it is quite acceptable to swear in her company, and never puts herself in a position where she might embarrass them. 'I don't go into the dressing room. No one has ever told me not to, but I don't because I don't think it is necessary.' She takes the jokes that come with being in charge of a group of boisterous men with good humour. Her first outing with the Under 21 international squad is a case in point. She was asked to take them to the cinema the day before a game in Brentford. So off they trooped: Michelle like a mother hen leading her brood through Slough town centre. 'Alan Shearer said: "Are you going to buy the popcorn then? The previous administrator always did," he whined. I stood there for a moment thinking, "Is he winding me up?" Thankfully I worked out he was,' she laughs.

## Gill Kilmartin – providing a home from home

Gill Kilmartin doesn't get to look after Alan Shearer's popcorn requirements; she cares for football's superstars of tomorrow. A landlady for Tottenham Hotspur, her large Victorian house in Bushy Hill, a north London suburb, is the first home away from home for up to three of the 16-year-old lads who sign on with the club straight from school. 'I hate to tell people what I do,' she says, 'because landladies have an image, don't they?' Well, Gill, 40, does not sport a blue rinse, an apron or rollers. Quite the opposite. She is trendy, says she can still remember what it's like to be young, and tries to reflect that in the way she takes care of her 'boys'.

'I certainly don't mollycoddle them, I'm more like a big sister than a surrogate mother,' she explains. 'I'm not the sort of landlady who is constantly at their beck and call. If they want a snack in the evening they can get it themselves, or if I'm busy and they want a shirt ironing, I'll point to the ironing board. It's good for them to learn to look after themselves.'

It can't be easy having three young, boisterous lads take over your home. 'It's not as bad as it sounds,' she laughs. 'We do have rules — no drinking, no wild parties — and I do try and encourage them not to stay out too late at night.' She has got used to the constant flow of girls who sit on her garden wall waiting for the boys. 'They seem to be extremely popular with girls, but as long as they go and chat to them outside the house I don't mind.' Because of their arduous training schedule at the club, the boys tend to be quite restrained at home. 'They come back and all they want to do is sleep, they're just not used to such constant physical exercise.'

It's the landladies who are out on the frontline when it comes to sorting out emotional problems, be it supporting the boys who aren't playing well, or those who are simply homesick. 'It's a very difficult time for them. They are not emotionally mature yet, so they're often a bit embarrassed to talk about their problems. I'm a mother myself, so I tend to know when something's wrong,' she

167

explains. The club doesn't encourage them to be open about their feelings. 'If you've got a problem: tough, just get on with it seems to be the attitude. The boys would never go and tell anyone at the club that they are homesick, because at the end of the day what are they going to do about it? It might backfire, be seen as a sign that they are not going to settle, so they probably won't want to say anything.'

'The club is so hard on them,' she says. 'I suppose they think it builds up stamina, but I do feel like saying sometimes: "Go easy on them, they may look like adults physically but they are really only just out of short pants."' She remembers one incident with a Spurs youth player on the verge of the first team. He had gone to stay with his girlfriend in Liverpool for the weekend. 'He had arranged it with the club. But I got a phone call from the club at 10 o'clock on Saturday morning saying they wanted him for the first team.' She did manage to get hold of him and he did get back on time. 'But the club were in a mad panic, ranting and raving: "Where is he?" "Why has he gone off to Liverpool?" They get sworn at and shouted at all the time.'

As a woman looking in on the masculine world of the football club, Gill thinks good communication and man-management skills are lacking. Take the way the boys who don't make the grade are discharged. 'When they are let go they are just told: "You aren't good enough." They don't try and break it to them gently. It's funny how they are treated. If there were more women involved in the running of clubs it wouldn't be like that. They would bring a softer approach,' Gill says. Consoling the boys who are let go – and most

**168**

are – is the worst part of being a landlady. 'It's heartbreaking because they all think they are going to be famous footballers. That's all they want to do.'

The club also overlooks practical matters. 'I often find myself doing things that the club could have helped with. No one tells the boys how to open a bank account or what a travelcard is. And it's things like this that make them feel uncomfortable. There's no reason why they should know these things – I didn't at that age.' Gill believes the club could put an induction pack together with factual information to help the youth players find their way around. There is only so much that Gill can do to give them the support that they need.

As a result of having the boys stay, her young son James is determined he wants to be a footballer when he grows up. But Gill is not so sure. 'It's a very competitive world. A player might just get himself established in the team and then get injured, and somebody else takes his place and he has to start all over again. There's a lot of frustration. And it can all so easily go wrong. A manager may not like your style of play and that's it, you're out,' and adds grimly, 'No, I hope he picks something else.'

behind the ball: giving the game a feminine touch

As these women show, given the opportunity, they can bring a freshness, a slightly different approach, to a predominantly male culture. Women are more approachable, less threatening, and in some cases, less dogmatic, more likely to weigh up options than assume it should be the way it has always been.

As Pat Smith puts it: 'Women are much better able to leave their egos out of the door. They don't come to meetings with a position, thinking: "This is my position. How can I defend it? They say: "How can we move forward? How can we get the best out of this situation?"'

Too often, women are still self-conscious about highlighting the positive qualities that they as women bring to the game – all the women interviewed said that they didn't want to make an issue of the fact that they are women. It is an understandable response to working in a male environment.

As Pam Burton, a director at Halifax Town put it in an interview for the Sir Norman Chester Centre for Football Research: 'It's the butch lady, isn't it? Nobody can equate femininity with authority, for some reason or other … If she's in power, then she's a lesbian, a dyke, whatever. And yet, a perfectly ordinary female is quite capable of having high authority and high power and not losing any of her characteristics … I think they'd bring a totally new perspective [more women directors]. I think the supporters would actually benefit more. I think they [women] see more, wider issues. I actually think the players, possibly, would benefit more as well, because you talk to them in a different way. You pick up on different aspects about them. You know more about their families quite often.'

While no woman should be expected to represent all women, they should not have to deny their sex. Too often, women in predominantly male fields adopt male patterns of behaviour because there are not enough women amongst them to make them feel easy about doing things differently. But it makes no sense, because women clearly do bring something beneficial to football. As football sociologist John Williams says: 'The downside of this approach is that it allows men to say: "Why can't all women be like her?", someone who stays in the background, who doesn't rock the boat. The great conundrum for women is how they can be true to their sex at the same time as adopting the proper requirements of their profession, which means doing things the way men have always done them.'

The prognosis can only get better for the women who have made that long march through football's male institutions. There are signs that the game is opening up, it is being feminized in a way that was inconceivable even five years ago. The evidence exists even in football's male heartland, in the fact that managers of the calibre of Chelsea's Ruud Gullit, Liverpool's Roy Evans and England's Glenn Hoddle are showing female traits in the way they organize and run their teams. As John Williams puts it: 'Theorizing about the game, displaying greater sensitivity in managing different kinds of people, recognizing that bawling at players isn't going to produce the best performance, getting to know something about a player's background and family,

learning about how to look after your body, these are all connected to female rather than male characteristics.'

It's a shift that is all for the good. Not only does it legitimize the
position of those women who work behind the ball, but it opens
the game up to new ideas. That can only make football a better
sport for everyone.

# Bird in the Box

## Tales from the Pressroom

It is 4.46 p.m. on Saturday and the first results come tripping out
of the teleprinter. Des, Trev, Gary and Stubbsy are familiar faces as
the post-match analysis begins to wind its way into the night. On
Radio 5 Live, David Mellor prepares to take up the mantle of voice
of the people on his regular 6.06 show. All very laddish.

But a quiet revolution is afoot. The lasses are hot on the heels of
media's lads. Take the football magazines: *90 Minutes*, which in
1997 merged with *Shoot*, was edited by a woman, Eleanor Levy,
while the first and easily the most successful of the new magazines,
*FourFourTwo* (80,000+ circulation), is run by its founding editor
Karen Buchanan.

The broadsheets, too, have seen an influx of new talent, with young
pretenders like the *Observer*'s Amy Lawrence and Emma Lindsey –
the first black female football writer – joining such legendary
veterans as Julie Welch. Even *Football Focus*, the preserve of suave
ex-pros, has its female face now, tough-talking Scot Hazel Irvine.
And on Radio 5 Live, the football fans' favourite station, Eleanor
Oldroyd and Charlotte Nicol pop up amongst the likes of Alan
Green and Mike Ingham.

# Julie Welch – first among unequals

It's a far cry from the days when Julie Welch, as a sports writer for the *Observer*, first walked into a press box in 1973. The striking scenes in her semi-autobiographical film, *Those Glory, Glory Days*, said it all: the dejected look on her face, no one to talk to, unable to get to a phone to put through her copy, she looked every inch the lone woman in a man's world.

Julie Welch remembers that time well. 'For the first few weeks everyone was very polite. They thought: "She'll go away soon." But when they realized I wasn't, they started to think: "What is this woman doing in our preserve?"'

Like many career women entering traditionally male occupations in the 1970s, she had opened up a Pandora's box of male anxiety. 'The press box was a closed male world,' she says, 'and very insecure. Even now, journalists are suspicious of newcomers because they are always worried someone else is going to take their job. The fact that it was an unknown woman dancing in there made them feel even more threatened.'

Then there was the publicity. She had become a product: 'Julie Welch first female football reporter', the subject of media profiles and interviews – she was even front page news. In an occupation where one's profile is jealously guarded, she was getting more than her fair share of attention, particularly for a young journalist just starting out. 'I was shameless about it,' she says. 'I courted it for all it was worth. And people didn't like that very much, so I learned to keep my head down after that.'

Many male journalists had never worked with a woman before and they had never expected to. As far as they were concerned, football was a man's game, run, supported and played by men. What on earth could a woman have to say about it?

In came Julie and knocked all their assumptions to the ground. Confident, intelligent and rather than being disgusted by the coarse, testosterone-soaked atmosphere of the sporting press box, like most women would, she thrived on it – just like them.

'I loved the job, that desperate act of getting your copy together on deadline, the adrenalin buzzing round, the feeling you get when you walk away from the ground and the story's in the bag. The old hunter-gatherer instinct has been satisfied.'

Even though Julie never set out to be a bra-burning feminist in the early 70s, that was how she came across. At a time when the women's liberation movement was demanding parity in the workplace and at home, when Angela Rippon had controversially become the first female newsreader, Julie appeared to be part of some great female revolt. 'People were always taken aback when they met me,' she laughs. 'Here I was, small, jolly, and very chatty, and they expected an enormous tub-thumper in boots.'

'Feminist' was not a label she ever sought, 'because people project so many things on to it that I didn't want. They'd think you hated men when in fact the opposite was true. I was drawn to the job because I liked male company – I always had.'

That was the reason she applied for the job as secretary to the sports editor of the *Observer* in the first place. 'I had a vague intention of becoming a journalist,' she explains (as a student at Bristol university she won the *Daily Telegraph* young journalist of the year award). 'It was only when I met these brilliant sports journalists I'd worshipped from reading the *Observer* – Hugh Mcilvanney, Arthur Hopcraft, Chris Brasher, Clem Thomas – that I thought: "I want to be like you."'

That and the realization that she was a terrible secretary. 'I never answered the phones, never booked anybody's press tickets. I thought it was beneath me. I had all the qualifications to be a hack: I was a lush, I'd spend all my time in the pub and I loved spending time with the boys talking about sport.'

Julie's big chance came in 1972 when Clifford Makins, the then sports editor, hung up his boots. His successor, later to become her husband, was impressed with a couple of feature ideas she put forward, and the fact that she had already written short stories and a couple of TV scripts. In 1973 she stopped being a secretary and was transformed into a football journalist. 'I thought people might be intrigued for half an hour, but there was quite an uproar – the idea of a woman writing about foot-ball. I never thought it was any big deal. But people did think it was unusual, they still do.'

She describes the first ten years of her football-reporting career as the loneliest of her life. Not only did the fact that she was the only woman mark her out as different, but also she was a single parent with a young son. Not an enviable position in a career renowned for its unsociable hours (a reason, Julie suggests, why so few female sports journalists have children).

'I couldn't afford childcare in those days,' she admits. 'I either had to abandon my son at home with strict instructions that he wasn't to go anywhere or answer the door, or I'd take him along to the match. If I couldn't get him a seat near the press box, I'd have to leave him out in the car, reading, while I reported the match and then dashed back to write my piece. But,' she adds with a wry smile, 'it did wonders for his education – he got A and S level English because he had to read so much.'

Julie's difficult situation did not provoke sympathy from one sports editor. 'Because I was rather poorly paid by the *Observer* and I had a son to support, I had to do all sorts of other work. He used to give me a hard time about all the other things I did, without giving me a real crack of the whip. I used to get fearfully upset. But a lot of women had to put up with that during the 1970s, without any form of redress. Despite that, the benefits always seemed to outweigh the disadvantages.'

Thankfully, things are better today. More women actually doing the job have brought weight in numbers. And a new generation of male sports writers are more open to the idea of working alongside women on an equal basis. 'It's still a male world but it's a much

**177**

nicer world, because you are part of the furniture,' Julie says. 'And if I've done nothing else, I've been responsible for getting women's toilets installed in the press box.'

## Second half, second wave

The new generation of female writers can only imagine what Julie Welch endured. As the *Observer*'s Amy Lawrence puts it: 'You have to prove your worth. But that goes for men and women. Once it's clear that you love the game and know what you are talking about, you will be taken seriously.'

*Sun* football writer Janine Self agrees: 'Journalists judge each other on actually doing a job. Once you are in that situation, they decide whether or not you are up to the task.'

I met 37-year-old Janine at the *Sun*'s Manchester office. Her desk was piled high with an assortment of shorthand notebooks, computer print-outs, the odd *Rothman's Year Book*, and that week's papers, upon which one of her two phones was precariously balanced. It rang intermittently throughout the interview. Behind that wall of sound and paper sat Janine. Slight and fey-looking, with wispy blonde hair and long tapering fingers, she looks too delicate to take on what must be the hardest job in sports journalism. How deceptive appearances can be.

Working on a tabloid is particularly difficult for a football writer, because so much of the job involves building and sustaining relationships with players and managers. Only then can you get those all-important exclusives that are the mainstay of the tabloid format.

'Men have so many advantages,' she explains. 'Most of the stories come from whispers in corridors. The lads get the big stories when they go out nightclubbing with the players, they are all "pals" together. If I go up to a player and suggest going out for a drink, it could be misinterpreted.'

Her view is that you have to be a realist. You have to accept that being a woman brings limitations. 'Anyone who says there aren't differences is living in a dream world,' she said, shrugging her shoulders. The point, however, is to get round them as best you can.

The one advantage a woman does have is that she stands out from the crowd, 'particularly if she looks a bit lost and lonely'. This fact might give a woman an opportunity to collar a player or manager first, or at least make it harder for him to refuse an interview. 'Men find it hard to be rude to women. So if a player doesn't want to talk to anyone after a game he would have no qualms about telling a man to get lost, but he won't say that to me.'

'I'm not saying,' she adds quickly, 'that you should go around wearing very short skirts or showing loads of cleavage, that would definitely rebound on you. But you do have to use the fact that you are a woman, the fact that you are more noticeable.'

Janine entered journalism – if not sports journalism – through conventional channels. She studied for her pre-entry qualification at the London College of Printing before moving to a weekly newspaper in Crawley, where she covered mainly news but occasionally deputized for the sports editor when he was on holiday. At that level, no one batted an eyelid.

But when she applied for a job as a sports writer on the *Morning Telegraph* in Sheffield – a large regional daily – she realized that it was unusual. 'There were lots of raised eyebrows when I arrived for the interview.' Indeed it did not seem the most promising of starts. The sports editor told her: 'I'm only interviewing you because the editor says I have to. I'm not going to offer you the job. I don't want a woman working on football.' Janine swallowed hard and figured it would be good practice anyway.

It was a most bizarre interview. 'We walked around Sheffield while he took his shoes to be resoled,' she explained. 'He actually interviewed me as we were walking along the Sheffield pavement.'

A week later he offered her the job. She believes he was so off-hand with her because he wanted to see if it would put her off, if she could cope with the sorts of prejudices that he knew would come her way. He knew how hard it would be.

'In the end,' Janine says, 'he was a bit over-protective. The first thing he told all the lads on the desk was not to swear in front of me. That wasn't very helpful because it just causes a situation where they will act differently towards you. If you're in a man's world you've got to let them act naturally.'

For female journalists on the broadsheets and magazines, the limitations are far less obvious. Broadsheets are interested less in exclusive news stories, and more in analysis, in-depth interviews, profiles and news features. Broadsheet journalists don't so much scrabble around for stories as comment on them.

Of course, building up contacts is still important. 'You do have to work harder to gain the respect of some players and managers,' says Amy Lawrence. 'They assume because you are a woman you don't know anything about football, that it's a waste of their time talking to you.'

Amy, 26, an Arsenal fan since she was in short socks, and a self-confessed anorak to boot, is supremely confident about her football credentials. 'I'll take anybody on, I'll ask them things they wouldn't even dream of,' she says, holding her hands up in a mock boxing pose. 'Come on, test me, test me.' She sees it as a challenge to change the minds of those who are a mite prejudiced against her.

'I interviewed Premier League chairman who would not look at me for the first 20 minutes. I was so obviously not going to under-stand a word he said. He was reading his letters, looking at his

**181**

diary, fiddling with his pen. He was really quite rude. But after half an hour he became more animated, and by the end he was extremely open. I'd obviously got through to him.'

Her method, she says, is 'always to drop in the odd fact, which isn't my job, but it shows that person that I know what I'm talking about, that I'm not just here for the ride.'

The idea that women don't understand football may be tiresome, but it can also bring unexpected rewards. 'You can sense a player or a manager is explaining things to you in a little more depth – more clearly even – because subconsciously they think you need the extra pointers. Sometimes you'll get better copy because they're saying things in their own language,' Amy explains.

They are equally liable to be slightly less guarded with a woman, in the sense that they don't expect a woman to catch them out, or they genuinely find women easier to talk to. 'On a number of occasions, players have said that when they are speaking to a male journalist, they put on their professional coat, and are very careful about what they say; they don't let themselves go. But with a woman they can be more easygoing. Maybe they trust a woman a little more. Well that's fine, as long as you don't go out with the intention of deceiving anybody.'

That, for Amy, is the bottom line. She would never abuse a position of trust by going into an interview with the express intention of either flirting with or schmoozing up to that person in order to get a better story. It is downright unprofessional and ultimately detrimental to all female journalists. It would just make all players and managers doubly suspicious of female journalists thereafter. Even if she did genuinely like a player, she would never let her feelings overstep the mark.

'It's a professional relationship,' Amy explains. 'I know that and the players know that. To an extent there might be a tension there, in a way that there wouldn't be if it was a chap doing the interviewing. Sometimes you get on well with people, sometimes you don't. But it's a working relationship. I've made some really good friends, we trust each other. That's nothing to do with fancying each other.'

## The female gaze

Many female journalists do believe they have a slightly different take on the game to their male counterparts. Janine Self's fellow football writer on the *Sun*, Vikki Orvice, says: 'You don't necessarily focus on the players, you don't go straight into the football, so you get a broader view. You write about what someone said on the way to the ground, the music that was playing, or something funny that happened.'

They are the mistresses of the human interest story. Julie Welch says that she 'writes with the novelist's ear and eye'; Amy Lawrence says that 'women are better on picking up aspects of personality'. While they inevitably bring this approach into writing match reports – Louise Taylor of the *Times* is noted for her quirky style, but also for being one of the best analysts of the game – it is in the feature

183

format that they excel. *The Daily Telegraph's* Sue Mott, 1996 feature writer of the year, Kate Battersby of the *London Evening Standard* and Julie Welch, now at the *Sunday Telegraph*, are all dab hands at interpreting that amorphous thing called mood. The feature format is an ideal place to pursue that style of writing.

As the coverage of football has increased at an incredible rate over the past few years, both within the regular sports pages of the national papers, and in the new weekly pull-out sports sections that newspapers like the *Sun*, *Independent* and *Guardian* publish – not to mention in the burgeoning number of football magazines – women have found more space in which to flower. Whereas once features were the marginal extras pushed in beside match reports – the so-called meat of sports journalism – today the keynote interview, the profile, and the full-length feature are the mainstays of any sports publication. And the rise of the feature has brought with it an increased profile for the female journalist.

Many female journalists suggest that men tend to be more interested in statistics and play down the human angle. While women may well ask players what they do in their spare time – taking the view that fans are interested in players – men, they suggest, are more likely to opt for quotes from the coaches, managers and chairmen.

The male obsession with statistics leaves many women cold. Perhaps it is because they did not grow up poring over *Rothman's Year Book*, as budding male journalists are likely to have done. Janine Self remembers her frustration as a child, that because she was a girl, she did not get access to those 'boys' books. 'My father

**184**

is very traditional, so my brother always got football books for Christmas, but I never did.' As it becomes more acceptable for women to like football, we will no doubt see a new generation of female Stattos – indeed we are perhaps beginning to already in the shape of young journalists like Amy Lawrence. The women who didn't have that early statistical induction had to find other ways of engaging with football and that may, in part, account for their different approach.

Julie Welch, however, puts it down to a more basic dissimilarity between men and women. 'Men seem to get this obscure pleasure out of seeing who can get the highest, the longest, which women don't get to the same degree. Men like the impersonality of numbers, measuring things. I suppose if you have a penis you've always got something to measure. Women don't have that. Women like to look at tactics and what shape the team plays in: is it the diamond formation, is there one lonely bloke up front, is it a Christmas tree? We like the whole body.'

Colin Gibson, sports editor of the *Sunday Telegraph*, who regularly employs half a dozen female journalists, puts their distinctive approach down to the way they are perceived by their peers. As he explained to Radio 4's Medium Wave listeners: 'The nickname that goes round the circuit is that they are fluffies, that they are light and bubbly and nice to look at, but there's no substance there. And they have to go through that process, they have to win that respect. But that helps because it makes them more determined. There is a pack and a herd mentality and you have to fit into that. And so some of the reports do become hackneyed, but that's something women don't have, because initially they find it hard to break into these packs … and while that's happening, they are writing from a different perspective and that gives them that freshness.'

Juliette Wills, until recently a staff writer on the football magazine *90 Minutes*, is disdainful of the pack mentality. She found out how it operates at close range when she travelled to Oslo as part of the official press corps, to cover England's pre Euro 96 game against the Norwegian national team. 'It was like being on the set of *Men Behaving Badly*,' she says mimicking the infantile actions of some of the male journalists, 'Stop the coach, I've got to go and get my mate out of the bar', 'Now look what you've done, you've broken my mobile phone.' She screams with frustration: 'Ahhh, it was like being in a zoo!'

Juliette tries to distance herself from the football herd at every possible moment. 'I want to produce the best story I possibly can, but because I write in a personal sort of way, I'm not going to get that by following the crowd.' So while all the other journalists were at the England team press briefing, Juliette was hiding behind a potted palm tree in the Norwegian team hotel (strictly out of bounds to English journalists), in an attempt to 'casually' bump into an unsuspecting Jan Fjiortoft, Norway's ace striker.

'I was laughing so much,' she says, glee emanating from her face, 'because all the other journalists were taking the mickey out of me. I hadn't been to any of the press briefings and they were obviously thinking: "She hasn't got a story, she hasn't done any interviews." Little did they know, I'd had a chat with Jan.'

**186**

'I like catching people unawares,' she says of her approach. 'That way you catch them off guard. If I could bungee jump in, I would.'

There is something incredibly charming about Juliette. She reminds you of a mischievous schoolgirl who bunks off school and never gets caught. You could imagine her sitting on the top deck of the school bus chewing gum and swooning over the pin-ups in *Jackie* magazine rather than agonizing over homework.

Indeed, she admits to having crushes on the players. There was a running joke in the *90 Minutes* office that should the occasion ever arise, they would put a splash on the cover 'Shock, horror, Juliette Wills interviews someone she doesn't fancy'. Juliette can't foresee her romantic notions abating just yet: 'Because even if a player isn't the best looking guy in the world, you can bet I will like him,' she explains. 'I just love footballers.'

Blushing a bright crimson – 'I know it's sick' – she recalls a dream she had recently about England international Robert Lee. 'He bought me a blue Ferarri with white leather seats [her team Spurs' colours] and we went for a drive along the Malibu coast. I've got a crush on him now. I've got millions of crushes. But if I didn't, my job wouldn't be half so exciting.' Yet she doesn't let her fantasies enter her writing. 'If anything I say sounds like I fancy a player, I take it out. That would just be too sad.'

Juliette does think that being a young woman makes it easier to get the big name interviews. 'Players enjoy being interviewed by a girl. I suppose it's a bit of a novelty, someone a bit different.' And it certainly makes approaching them less troublesome. 'After a game, I just go up and say: "Hi, I'm Juliette. Can I be really cheeky – I don't want to interview you now, but can I have your number and give you a ring?" I could be some girl off the street for all they know. But they never question it, they simply think: "It's a bird, alright then." If I was some 50-year-old hack, they'd be more wary.'

The very fact that she gets so flustered around her idols and inevitably 'goes really, really red', does, she claims, help her to get a better interview. Although there is nothing fake about the blushes, it puts people at their ease. 'You can literally see them relax. Sometimes they'll say: "Look, it's OK, it's only me."'

Perhaps the players feel flattered that an attractive young woman is so in awe of them – all journalists feel the same about some particular player, but most keep it to themselves – and it just makes them open up. 'If they are still a bit uptight or holding back, I'll say: "You can tell me, I won't put it in," and I wouldn't. If they say anything that is the least bit dodgy or makes them look really stupid, then I'll keep it. I don't expect a player to be a literary star. In fact, if they haven't done a very good interview, I'll tell them them as much but I'll say: "It's OK, I'll make you sound more interesting." And they'll be like: "Oh god, thank you."'

Juliette is a fan first and foremost. While she admits it would be easy to become cynical –'you hear about players moving clubs just to get their signing on fees' – she doesn't let it affect her too much. 'I love the excitement you feel as a fan. The day I lose that is the day

**188**

I'll stop, and I want to convey that feeling to the reader. After all, fans don't want to have their idols smashed to pieces.'

This approach coming from a young woman who is of a similar age to many of the players has led to misunderstandings. Juliette is now close friends with a one time interviewee, Blackburn's Gary Croft. So well did they get along at the interview that Gary's then girlfriend was convinced they were having an affair. Even his father 'and everyone at his local' were speculating. 'It wasn't true,' she giggles, 'but so strong was the rumour, I had to put in my article: "Angie [the said girlfriend's name], I'm not having an affair with Gary, OK."'

According to Juliette, the very idea was preposterous. Angie, 'a blue-eyed blonde in baby-doll dresses, is the typical player's girlfriend, and I'm just not like them'. But it doesn't stop girlfriends like Angie feeling threatened. 'You do get that sometimes. A girlfriend will look you up and down in the players' lounge after the game, you can tell they are thinking: "Who is this?" or secretly wishing you were 18 stone.'

However, Juliette has learned to be more tactful. 'I always make it clear to wives that I'm not after their husbands,' she says. 'When I phone up to speak to a player, I always tell them straightaway that I'm a journalist, so they know I'm not some mysterious girl. I know how they must feel at the thought of someone being after their husband.'

Having crushes on players, however innocent, does, Juliette admits, lend itself to a slightly different journalistic approach. 'It would be the same if men were reporting on netball.' Male journalists may

189

be just as in awe of their heroes, but they seek to impress them by proving how knowledgeable they are about the game. 'Me,' Juliette says, 'I'm the inquisitive female fan who wants to find out as much as possible about her idol. I'm more of a delver.'

## Going glossy – the magazine women

It is no surprise then that Juliette Wills should have gravitated towards *90 Minutes*. Although in May 1990, *90 Minutes* was forced to merge, due to falling sales, with that other long-standing football magazine *Shoot*, it will nonetheless be remembered as one of the first publications to inaugurate a new, disrespectful, popish approach to the game. Launched in 1990, it was concerned with the passions that football inspires. It didn't carry match reports or concentrate on the tactics on the pitch. 'We were interested in the fans' experiences, what it's like to be watching in the pub or sitting in an armchair, shouting at the referee, arguing amongst yourselves, laughing at Darren Peacock's hair – all the things fans do,' says then editor Eleanor Levy, the first female editor of any national football publication, now editor of *Shoot*.

Journalists on *90 Minutes* wrote as fans rather than neutral observers. 'I don't want to go in the press box and watch Manchester United,' says Eleanor, a longstanding Spurs fan. 'I want to go in the same stand I've been going to for the past seven years and watch my team.'

This approach opened up the football media to a generation of journalists – women included – who never dreamt they could be sports writers. 'When I was growing up, I didn't think newspapers employed women sports journalists, and I was never confident enough to want to do anything groundbreaking,' she says.

*90 Minutes'* writers were as interested in pop culture as sport. Many, like Eleanor, are ex-music journalists, 'who grew up reading *NME'*, and relished the challenge of 'writing about football in the same way they would a music feature'.

Aimed at a 20-something audience – although many readers are teenagers – *90 Minutes* showed 'a completely different side of the players. 'They are featured talking about fashion, music and girls as much as football.' Some managers were shocked at what they read. 'They were not used to seeing players described this way,' Eleanor explains. 'They are used to years of Harry the hack hanging out with footballers, watching them play and only using selected highlights of what they say. But the old guard in football – be it managers or administrators – are going to have to realize that there is a different breed of journalists commenting on the game now.'

And the fact that women are amongst them is no big deal? 'On *90 Minutes* you didn't feel part of a hard-pressed minority. Everyone talked about football, what they saw on TV, and music. Gender just didn't enter into it.'

She believes that that goes for younger players too: the biggest tension is generational rather than gendered. 'Players enjoy talking to journalists of their own age – male or female – rather than some 50-year-old hack in a bad suit. They've just got more in common.

The fact that you are female increasingly doesn't get you noticed because there are so many women coming through.'

Formed in 1994, *FourFourTwo* was the brainchild of another woman. Karen Buchanan was a latecomer to the joys of football. She only got hooked during the 1990 World Cup, along with 14 million other women. 'I always thought football was not targeted at me when I was growing up,' she explains. 'But I was converted by Italia 90. It was wonderful, a pantomime for grown-ups. It touched patriotic bits I never knew I had. I came away thinking: "This game for lager louts is quite a laugh – it's passionate and brilliant."'

So inspired was she that she came up with the idea for a new kind of football magazine. With its glossy format, in-depth features and smattering of terrace humour, it aims to provide serious and challenging reading for an adult audience.

'Because I came to football without a great deal of background knowledge, I wanted a magazine that would help me analyse the issues, put things in a context and keep me informed, as well as being a good read,' Karen says.

What she recognized was that there were a good many other women just like her. Post-1990 football underwent an image change and a massive popularity explosion. It became hip to be a football fan. People who had only a cursory interest were suddenly looking at the game with fresh eyes. They were one of the markets *FourFour Two* tapped into.

'The football audience is far more diverse than the traditional image of the white working class man. There are just as many people, including women, picking up *FourFourTwo*, who haven't been to a game for years, but are interested in football,' Karen explains.

With its comprehensive range of statistics and information, lengthy interviews and journalistic coups – it managed to get Terry Venables as guest editor – it appeals not only to the football obsessive but new supporters, greedy to digest those essential facts that still define the 'real' fan. After reading *FourFourTwo*, a 'fledgling female fan could go into a pub and have a conversation with her boyfriend, confident she knows what she's talking about,' Karen says. It doesn't take swathes of background knowledge for granted or make oblique references that only the 'true' supporter would know.

With a female editor, assistant editor and production editor, women have a high profile within the magazine. 'It wasn't a PR stunt,' Karen insists. 'They were the best candidates for the job.' But it does send out positive signals that women can and do write knowledgeably about football.

**193**

While *FourFourTwo*'s audience is still predominantly male, 12 per cent of its readers are women – more than any other football magazine and the same percentage as the number of fans who attend Premier League games. 'We don't make any reference to whether someone is male, female, young or old – it's a magazine for everyone.' But it does have a tacit policy of not alienating women readers by selling itself using the laddish 'tits and arse' approach of some of its competitors. It is not overtly boysy.

Karen says that women supporters 'want to be treated not as "female fans", but simply as fans. We wouldn't have a separate page for women, because that would be patronizing. It would be like saying: "Here's the page for women, and the rest is for men, because women are obviously stupid and can't understand the proper news."'

Given its strong female editorial presence, you might expect that women's football would get plenty of coverage in *FourFourTwo*'s pages. But this is not the case. 'While it's great to see women's football taking off,' Karen says, 'we would never cover it, because it's just not the same game. We are writing about a game that has a huge structure in place and a massive following – a completely different game, if you like. For us to cover women's football would be as bizarre as if we were to write about rugby football.'

**194**

# Fanzines don't have to be manzines

Commercial magazines are not the only publications that put forward a fan's eye view of football. Go to any league game and you will see a solitary figure standing by the gates of the ground, carrier bag stuffed full of photocopied sheets, shouting: 'Get your Brian Moore's Head/Up the Arse/Fortune's Always Hiding' (the list is endless). Produced on a shoestring, fanzines are part of an alternative culture that emerged in the mid-80s and 10 years later remains, on the surface, as strong as ever. They are produced by fans themselves as an alternative to the bland club magazines that rarely criticize the actions of the chairman, manager or board of directors. In order to produce these labours of love you need to be fanatical – think of all the hours spent stapling pages together. And you need to be fanatical to read them.

They are alternative without being avowedly politically correct: anti-commercialization, champions of the rights of fans and, on occasions, campaigners against the terrible twins, racism and sexism. While alternative, they are generally produced by men. Just like trainspotters, programme collectors, and music fans who desperately hunt out that obscure record from their favourite band, fanzine writers and readers are generally male. It is ironic that this culture with progressive aims should be so overwhelmingly male. However, as in many sections of male culture, there is a female presence.

Sue and Dave Wallis are joint editors of the Manchester City fanzine, *King of the Kippax*. Sue and Dave started *King of the Kippax* in 1988, at a time when the image of football fans was at an all-time low. Football fans were commonly perceived as hooligans, a menace to decent society. 'We felt the views of the ordinary fan weren't being heard,' Sue says. 'We were sick of being treated like cattle at games, herded along by police, having our complaints ignored by the club, putting up with terrible facilities. And we wanted to say that – that football fans aren't yobs and animals.'

Produced from their spare room, *King of the Kippax* is a family affair. Dave writes the match reports, Sue draws the cartoons, Sue's 80-year-old mother does the typing, and all the family come home on match days to help sell it. 'It keeps us together as a family. I've got grown-up children who have their own lives now, but the fanzine is something we have in common.'

It does bring its fair share of family disharmony as well. 'Dave is so intense about football,' Sue laughs, 'so the fanzine has to be just the way he wants it. I would like the cartoons to be more vicious but Dave won't have that, they're his heroes and he doesn't like me having a go. I don't mind really, I know how much it means to him.'

**196**

Sue describes herself as a latecomer to football – she has only been going since she met Dave 33 years ago. 'I'm not as analytical as Dave,' she explains. 'I don't have the background he does – Dave used to write match reports in his scrapbook as a little lad.'

'I write as the wife of a fan, the mother of a fan, because that's my experience. That's all I can do. I'm not very good at writing about football itself, because I haven't got that sort of way of looking at it. I did a match report once and Dave said: "You didn't say who scored the goal." But I didn't think it was relevant. I was writing about the atmosphere, the little incidents that happened, what people had said, because who scored the goal was in the evening paper.

'We have a young girl who writes for the fanzine who reads the game like men do. That's not common for women, though I think that will change as more girls go to games early on.'

Sue would like to see more women writing for *King of the Kippax*. 'I have asked women to put what they say in writing, but they don't, partly because they are less confident. Men just assume they know about football, they've usually played and watched it since they were kids. Women haven't had that headstart.'

Getting more women writers isn't a particular policy of the fanzine. '*King of the Kippax* isn't aimed at either men or women – it's aimed at City fans. There is no feminist streak in it. It's irrelevant whether you are black, white, male or female. Sometimes Dave writes sexist things and I type it and then make a little remark.'

197

Indeed, Sue says women don't want to be singled out as a minority, or put under pressure to write from the perspective of the female fan. 'Women will write in their own good time,' she says, 'and they want to write as fans – nothing more.' When they do, it may well have a radical edge. 'Men are more traditional, they hang onto their little boy images of the terraces and good old days. Women are more receptive to change – we want modernization from the toilets upwards.'

Jane Hart is certainly one woman who wants to shake things up. Editor of the Wimbledon fanzine *Sour Grapes*, she's involved in a war of words with the local supporters' club. 'Some of the people there just don't seem to have any go,' she says in her clipped home counties accent. 'They've been doing the job for so long, they've got comfortable. Why aren't they out campaigning for a new ground?'

The trouble started when she wrote an article in the supporters' club magazine, *Wandering Hans*, criticizing the supporters' club's travel arrangements. 'We travelled to a game against Leeds and came back via Manchester. Three times we went round that city before the driver admitted he'd lost his way.' She throws her hands up in the air in frustration. 'Lost his way? He was incompetent. And I said so.' Two months later the editor was expelled from the supporters' club, a month later her husband followed, and Jane was on the warpath. 'It was obviously because of what I wrote,' she says.

'Someone had to tell the world what had happened so I started *Sour Grapes*, thinking it would be a one-off. And people wrote in saying: "Please carry on," so I've been doing it ever since.'

A house mistress at a boys' public school in Surrey, Jane is used to jaws dropping when she says she edits a football fanzine. But 'the boys at school think it's marvellous, it's done wonders for my popularity,' she says. 'They call me "the posh tart who goes to football", which isn't so bad considering what they could say.'

*Sour Grapes* is a sort of *Daily Telegraph* of its genre. No split infinitives, sloppy sentences or spelling mistakes here. But it is very funny. 'Some fanzines are fairly scurrilous. A fanzine should be a bit of fun, a quirky eye view of football. I do bring out the naffness quite often,' she says.

Jane writes her own column, 'Woman in the Stand', where she loves to play to the gallery, writing some of the things supporters expect from female supporters. 'My fans expect it of me,' she says, tongue in cheek. 'Men aren't so honest about their feelings. I will say what I really feel. I do put the sexist bit in. When Reg Davies [the commercial manager] jumped up and showed his braces [at a supporters' meeting] I wrote this piece about him strutting his stuff, which Reg thought was wonderful. The great sex symbol of Wimbledon, forget Dean Holdsworth, here's Reg.'

199

Off the page, Jane thinks supporters find her easier to approach because she is a woman. 'I do find that when I'm selling the fanzine, I become an agony aunt. People come up and say: "I had terrible trouble getting in today," or "I haven't got my away tickets," as if I'm supposed to sort out all their problems. Some bloke came up and said: "The marriage is off." I didn't even know it was on. They look towards me as the woman of the people to write things, so I think I'm fairly accessible.'

Jane has that bossy schoolmarmish tone that sends hapless officials running for cover. The fanzine is full of her run-ins with the great and good of football. The time she wrote to Everton director Bill Kenwright 'about the disgraceful behaviour' of racist Everton fans. 'He phoned back and said how sorry he was.' So Jane told him the only way he would get round it was to sign some black players. She giggles: 'They signed Amokachi soon after.'

What she has received the most flack for are her views on Wimbledon's male supporters. 'I've never noticed any sexism at Wimbledon, perhaps I've become an honorary bloke,' she says, 'so I wrote about how the male fans were very nice and how I felt safe with them.' Low and behold, even Wimbledon's notoriously middle class, well educated male supporters took umbrage, which does show just how much men affirm a macho image through football. One man wrote in response: 'Of course we're sexist, who does she think she is?'

# On the fairwaves

Charlotte Nicol was convinced that the millions of regular listeners
to Radio 5 Live were thinking: 'Who does Charlotte Nicol think she
is?' when in 1990 she became the first female football broadcaster
on national radio. 'There was this stigma, you just felt people were
at the ends of their radios gasping: "It's a woman."'

I met Charlotte, now the football producer at Radio 5 Live, in the
press lounge at Millwall football club. It wasn't quite a case of
spittoons in every corner and sawdust on the floor, more like a
betting shop with carpets, as a scores of raincoat-clad men watched
*Football Focus* on the overhead TV or joked amongst themselves.
An hour before the game, Charlotte was the only female sports
journalist there.

Not that she minds, she is used to it. But it can cause the odd
'hilarious' misunderstanding. Charlotte recalls attending a press
lunch at Chelsea football club. 'I went up to the main door and
Ken Bates, the chairman, was there. "Are you here for the press
lunch or to serve the drinks?" he asked.'

Wrapping her grey coat with a black fur collar around her, Charlotte
didn't look like she was about to take up smoking cheroots to adapt
to the male atmosphere. 'I don't minimize the fact that I'm a woman,
but neither would I play the helpless bimbo, there's no need for it,'
she explains. 'I'm no shrinking violet or delicate girl – I never have
been, I've always been one of the lads.'

**201**

But aged 18 and applying for journalism college, Charlotte wasn't at all sure she could become a football lass. 'I said I wanted to be a football writer, and the tutors just fell about laughing, which was justified, because the only female football writer then was Julie Welch.'

In fact Charlotte fell into football reporting by accident. She worked for an independent radio station in the Northeast. 'When they realized I was interested in sport, they decided to send me to interview the then Middlesbrough manager Bruce Rioch. And I thought: "This is it, I've found my niche." But it wouldn't have occurred to me to ask at that point because I just didn't think it was an option. Sport was very male.

'The biggest hurdle was that you just didn't know what you were capable of. There were no guidelines, no one saying: "Look, this is how I did it," so you didn't know what to aim for. If I could go back and do it all again I would do things differently. I would make myself do commentary, I would make myself play the game – even though I'm no sportswoman. But at the time I didn't think to do that because no woman had. So you are up against mental barriers.'

Even five years ago, Charlotte never dreamt she would become the football producer – one of the top jobs in Radio 5 Live's sportsroom. There was a feeling that a woman couldn't do the job because the football producer needs access to the tunnel – the engineers have their position inside it – and she might see naked players. 'There were rumours that Gazza used to go tearing out of the dressing room with nothing on.'

'I keep a low profile,' Charlotte says. 'I wouldn't want someone lurking outside my dressing room, so I am discreet.' Has being a woman caused any problems? 'No,' she laughs, 'I've only seen one bum in five years – and that was in my private life.'

The one area where women have still to make a breakthrough is in the field of commentating. There are no budding Alan Greens or Bob Wilsons on the horizon. Charlotte puts it down to a 'lack of opportunities for women at a local level. If women don't get pushed through there, then they can't go on to do it at a national level.' But even if a woman did come through, it would be a daunting prospect. It's the rubicon yet to be crossed. 'There would be so much pressure on the first woman commentator, she really would be exposed to criticism.' With a perceptible shiver, Charlotte adds: 'Thank god, it won't be me.'

Charlotte's Radio 5 Live colleague, Eleanor Oldroyd, would also like to see more women sports journalists developing their talents in local radio. 'You need to have a strong skills base,' she explains.

It is a route Eleanor has travelled herself. She started off as a sports producer at Radio Shropshire: 'I learned how to broadcast and I learned about sport before I became a broadcaster on national radio.'

That experience has taken her a long way: in 1996 she fronted *Sport on 5*, Radio 5 Live's principal Saturday afternoon sports show. *Sport on 5*, together with its predecessor, *Sport on 2*, has been BBC radio's flagship sports show for 50 years. Since its inception in 1947, no woman apart from Eleanor has presented it. Her other credits

**203**

include presenting Radio 5 Live's *Women on Top*, a programme for women who play sport, *Sunday Sport* and the station's *Breakfast News* sports bulletins.

What worries her is the tendency on the part of some broadcast editors to want women to report on football simply because they are women: the 'we ought to get a woman doing this' syndrome, because it's trendy to do so.

'It is encouraging if people are more open-minded,' she says. 'It's certainly helped me. I've probably ended up doing lots of things I couldn't have done 10 years ago because they wanted to keep the male representation going.

'There's also a danger that you end up with people who don't know as much as they might do. When I came into the Radio 5 Live sports room I knew quite a bit about sport, but I had a lot of catching up to do. You need to learn the ropes, and that doesn't come overnight.

'There is a danger that token women are brought in and get caught out. Women have to be very careful about making mistakes because we are judged more harshly. And women who don't know what they are talking about may end up spoiling it for everyone else. People say: "Oh, she's a woman and she doesn't know anything about football," ergo women don't know anything about football.' "

Eleanor admits she still gets 'slightly sweaty palms' when she's reporting a match on a Saturday afternoon. 'You know you've got to get it right because there are millions of people listening to you. The pace is so quick, every 10 minutes you are on air, and you've got to do a 10 second report, starting with the score and ending with the summing up.' It's not like the print media, where journalists have a press conference with the manager after the game, 'so they have a bit more time,' Eleanor says.

'It's fantastic when you get it right, but most games I come away thinking: "I could have done that better." I imagine all these people sitting in their cars driving home and saying "I can't believe she was at the same game as us."

'You feel it more as a woman, because you have more to prove. You are much more under the critical eye of people. If you say something wrong, they'll say: "That's what happens when you send a woman along." Whereas the guys I'm sure make mistakes, but people don't question it.

'I always feel really churned up if I get something wrong, or if I've missed an instant, which is easy to do if you take your eye off the game and suddenly someone's down on the floor writhing in agony. Which is why when you go in the press box you hear: "Who hacked him down?" or "Who put the cross in?", but if you are a woman you feel slightly self-conscious about asking, because they are going to say: "Oh god, she wasn't watching, typical." It is very exciting and I love doing it but it's very nerve-wracking.'

# The Des, Trev, Gary ... and Hazel show

Radio is not the only broadcast medium to have employed more women over the last five years. The number of women sports journalists working in television has also increased.

The woman who has been broadcasting on television for longer than anyone else is Hazel Irvine. A national institution in Scotland, she's a regular sports correspondent on BBC Scotland's evening news programme *Reporting Scotland*, and also the first female football reporter on *Football Focus*. As if that's not enough, she has also been known to present *Sports Scene*, the Scottish equivalent of *Match of the Day*.

Hazel puts her success down to being an active sportswoman right up to leaving university. Not football mind, but hockey, swimming, athletics and golf. While many male journalists believe you have to have played football yourself to understand it, Hazel says that by playing any ball game 'you develop the same tactical awareness. In hockey, you've got five forwards across the front, you're playing in exactly the same way. It's a mirror image of what's happening in football.'

It's not just the tactics – which she admits, when you give a 30–45 second piece to camera, you are not going to be able to expand upon at any length – it's the fact that if you love sport yourself, you can convey that excitement to the audience. 'I feel a real enthusiasm for all sports because I've got so much enjoyment out of playing it. And you can't manufacture that love.'

206

With a whole channel dedicated to sport, Sky TV is the channel for most serious sport lovers. Because of its sheer volume of football coverage, Sky Sports needs a variety of forms of presentation. This makes it far more female-friendly than its terrestrial rivals. From straight match reports and commentary on games, to shows that have selected managers discussing tactics, to shows specifically for fans to sound off, it makes football seem more open and accessible. Even the coverage of games is done in an imaginative way, with attractive camera angles that evoke some of the aesthetic presentation that was so attractive to women during Italia 90.

Opening up the game is something that Emily Boulting believes is very important. A former producer on Sky Sports' *Soccer AM*, a show hosted by Russ Williams and Helen Chamberlain which goes out on Saturday and Sunday mornings, and which is aimed at fans, Emily says that 'you have to take into account that people come to football with different degrees of knowledge.'

Indeed, the Head of Programming at Sky recognized that himself when his son, aged 11, who was watching TV asked him: 'Did Kevin Keegan play football?' 'It really brought home to him,' Emily explains, 'that there will always be new people who don't know the "obvious".' She adds: 'Maybe that's why someone like me is suited to this show, because I don't know that much.'

*Soccer AM* is an entertainment-led magazine show – although both Russ and Helen are avid football fans – with fun items. After Paul Gascoigne had his hair bleached white, they had a top hairdresser from Toni and Guy on the show to produce some stylish football haircuts. They respond to viewers, such as the five-year-old boy who claimed he could tell any football player by looking at his legs, so they had a flip card of legs for him to guess the player. Its aim is not to talk over anyone's head.

That is not to decry the contribution of other more fact-based pro-grammes, where a greater degree of knowledge is assumed, but to make the point that they can co-exist, providing a range of coverage. 'Other shows enjoy that exclusivity,' Emily says, 'which is more suited to men, but not every show has to do that.'

Emily, a former drama student, believes that you can appeal to a wide cross-section of fans by bringing out the drama and humour of football. And in 29-year-old Helen Chamberlain she has someone who has the warm, vibrant personality to do just that. Helen is a dyed-in-the-wool Torquay fan, travelling two hundred odd miles to home games every other week straight after *Soccer AM* has finished.

'I'll be there with my bongo drums,' she says, 'tapping out tunes from Bananarama and Funboy Three to get the atmosphere going.' She enjoys football for the laughs and camaraderie rather than the offside rule or the sweeper system. She has no hang-ups about that. 'A lot of girls feel they have to prove themselves, but I don't. You shouldn't have to justify why you like something,' she says.

She started working in television on Sky's children's channel, Nickelodeon, where she was always talking about football. Indeed, she brought the footballing dilemmas she faced in her own life into

**208**

the show. 'I had a boyfriend who asked me to go to a wedding on a Saturday and I was in a real quandary. It was really important to him that I went but it meant missing Torquay away at Walsall. I honestly didn't know what to do. So I explained my situation on the show and got the kids to phone in and tell me what to do. Inevitably all the kids said: "Go to football," except one little lad who was most disgruntled: "I think it's disgusting. Why should you go and enjoy yourself? If it was the other way round you would expect your boyfriend to go with you,"' Helen said giggling. In the end she did go to the game, even though she had told her boyfriend she would go to the wedding. 'I got in the car intending to go to the wedding but before I knew it I was on the motorway heading north.' It was the end of that relationship, not that Helen minded too much. 'He reckoned he was an Arsenal fan,' she explained, 'but I went round to his house one evening when Arsenal were playing Manchester United, and he didn't even know they were playing. He was watching *The Bill*.

'I love being a presenter, although I send myself up something rotten. If I don't know the answer to some statistical question I'll say: "What do you expect? I'm a blonde." I don't mind that. Football isn't rocket science, it's fun. And the best part is that no one fan has all the answers.'

Twenty-four years ago Julie Welch started a shift in journalism that has proved irreversible. It's not just fighting for space and it's not just giving that feminine feel-good colouring in the background that women journalists in all fields are expected to contribute. It's a combination of both.

Much as the lads would hate to admit it, this transformation in football reporting, away from a traditional men only world of win, lose or draw, makes the game more interesting for everyone. When a black dreadlocked Dutchman takes over from a dour Scottish centre half as the nation's favourite football pundit, and holds even his fellow presenters in silent awe of his eloquence, then we are all witnessing how the outsider opens up the inside for all of us.

This is what Eleanor Oldroyd, Jane Hart, Janine Self and others of their ilk are giving to football.

one of the lads

# Conclusion

## The Missionary Position

Women fans have a part to play in football's future. If football clubs and supporters are astute, it won't be a part on the margins of the game, as the woman on the arm of her boyfriend or as the glamorous model donning football kit to advertise the Carling Premiership 'Get Your Kit Off' game in a link-up with the *Sun*. Women, given the opportunity, have a much more central role to play in the future of the game, that could reap benefits both for the clubs themselves and for fans who are committed to securing football's status as a live, spectator experience.

That women are good for football's image is an idea that has credence amongst the more strategically-minded observers of the game. Sociologist John Williams, for example, remarks that: 'their increasing presence diminishes the game's aggressive and macho image'. Women could be a big help in the refashioning of the game that the football clubs and authorities are so actively pursuing. Why then has so little been done to woo women fans?

There has only been one national initiative to actively target women fans and that was organized by the FA in the run up to England hosting the 1996 European championships, Euro 96. It was an imaginative and welcome campaign. Aimed at young women – the ads appeared in the pages of the glossy magazines *Elle*, *Cosmopolitan*, *Marie Claire* and *Options* – it exactly caught the self-confident, independent and aspirational mood of young women today. 'How can I lie back and think of England when Venables hasn't finalized the squad?', '"You'd rather spend next June going to see football than going on holiday? I don't believe it," he said', were just two of the captions that accompanied images of strong, sexy women – all football fans in their own right – who stared out of the pages alone – rather than being portrayed as bimboesque male accessory items.

The message was clear: being a female football fan doesn't mean you have to leave your femininity or your independence at home. The campaign also reflected the reality that the fastest growing group of fans are young, single women. Given the viewing figures for Euro 96, there is a potentially huge, untapped audience of female fans out there, waiting to be captured by their local club. Sponsorship Research International found that men made up 55 per cent of the those who watched Euro 96 on TV, women 45 per cent. And 93 per cent of men claimed to have watched at least 30 minutes of any one game compared to 76 per cent of women.

The problem with the FA's campaign was that it was not part of any consistent strategy. David Davies, the FA's head of public affairs, recognized the importance of reaching out to new constituencies when he said: 'Much has been written about bringing families back to football. Actually, that's nonsense. Families never went to football – only fathers and sons. It's our job to attract families,

212

so women have to be a particular target to broaden our audience.'
All well and good, but after Euro 96, the FA's attempt to broaden
football's audience was effectively put on the back burner.

Helen Willis, marketing and PR coordinator of Euro 96, explained the
FA's position thus: 'Euro 96 provided us with a unique opportunity
to do something we have wanted to do for a long time, namely
welcome women to football. Here we had an event that, just like
Italia 90, offered all the drama and passion of top class football in
some of England's best stadia. What we wanted to say to women
who had not been to a game before, or not for a long time, was:
"Come along, it's not intimidating, it's not dangerous and it's not
just for men."' But, as Helen goes on to explain, the continuing
specific promotion of football to women is not on the immediate
agenda. 'In terms of advertising on behalf of individual clubs after
the tournament, that is not part of our brief. We administer national
events. It is down to individual football clubs to then advertise
themselves to new fans. But that may make sense, there are no
doubt women out there who have enjoyed the tournament and who
would like to follow a team but who don't have a club they identify
with. Clubs may do well to advertise themselves to these women.'

This response is not good enough. If the football authorities don't
take a lead and provide the support and the infrastructure for
actively reaching unrepresented audiences, who will? Standing
alone, it's no surprise that the clubs who can afford to promote
themselves to new fans – the big Premier League heavyweights
such as Manchester United, Newcastle, Arsenal and Liverpool –
say they don't need to make new fans. It is in the lower divisions –

in the Nationwide League and the non-league clubs – that specific attempts have been made to attract women: Blackpool, for example, offers cut-price tickets for women on Mother's Day. But these clubs tend to be the ones that don't have the resources to promote themselves week in week out.

How different the situation might be if the FA, together with the Premier and Football Leagues, was willing to organize a campaign across the divisions they administer, to encourage women to go to games. With the backing and prestige that the big clubs could offer, such a campaign would benefit the smaller clubs with the space to accommodate new fans. It needs a national governing body like the FA to coordinate such an initiative.

Why can't the footballing authorities finance a campaign aimed at getting fans to take their mothers, and mothers who already go to take their daughters, to a game on Mothering Sunday? Given that there is virtually always a Sky game on a Sunday, it's an initiative that Sky may well pick up on because it would be in their interests too to draw in more female viewers. And how about initiating a campaign around Valentine's Day or International Women's Day aimed at getting women along to games? Some might claim such campaigns smack of tokenism. A more positive way of looking at it is to say that it gives a constituency previously excluded from football a foot in the door.

Even for the big clubs it makes sense to be constantly thinking in terms of reaching out to new constituencies. Precisely because football clubs are now businesses, run according to the laws of the market rather than the rules of the game, it is vital that they constantly build and rebuild a strong fan base. Fans buy tickets – that ticket income may not be as substantial as the revenue clubs can now accrue from sponsorship or TV deals, but it is still significant; they buy merchandise; their presence attracts club sponsors; they buy shares in their clubs. These forms of revenue are important and could be increased still further if there were more fans.

But football clubs tend to think that fans are born, not made. So while some attempt to attract families to games by offering cut price tickets in the family enclosures for certain games, in the main, it is only those fans who are already going to games who are aware that this initiative exists. It's a good endeavour but it is preaching to the committed rather than reaching out to potential new fans.

Clubs need to use the most modern and sophisticated marketing techniques to reach new fans and bring them into the game. They can't take it for granted that people who aren't born into football-following families will automatically find their way into the ground.

Making fans means using a whole range of ways in which people can attach themselves to their club. This would require clubs to build up a far more holistic relationship with the local community. More clubs could, for example, offer family open days, so that local people could come and look round the club that exists right in the heart of their locality and takes the name of its neighbourhood, town or city. In far too many cases clubs have none but the most cursory of links to that place. It would be an opportunity for those outside to familiarize themselves with the club, see how it operates and realize that they too could find a niche within its walls. And how about clubs offering keep fit classes, aerobics, Weight-watchers' evenings or mothers' and toddlers' clubs? Not as optional extras, but because building an ever-expanding range of attach-ments and ways of identifying with the club could broaden its fan base – by making new fans – as well as deepening fan loyalty by giving something back to existing supporters.

Football has to come to terms with the fluidity of the 'masses' that will provide its future support. In the modern 'society of choice' – particularly in the context of an expanding leisure sector – football cannot assume that its current pre-eminence as the biggest live spectator sport will remain unrivalled, nor can it be sure that a natural constituency exists as if by right. The kids of today – and the fans of tomorrow – are as likely to sink their money into Nintendo computer games as they are to kick a football around. So to protect its long-term future, football has to constantly rebuild its fan base.

But satisfying the desires of the burgeoning female audience that would surely be at the centre of any outreach strategy, necessitates a change in the ways clubs conduct their relationships with fans. This change needs to reflect an acceptance that not all fans are the same, that they have different needs, emotional attachments, and degrees of loyalty. Such a sea-change in attitudes will not only serve women and other new, untapped audiences well – in particular the ethnic minorities who are so seriously under-represented in the stands compared to their presence on the pitch – but football's traditional source of support too: the inner-city working class who are currently being forced out of the game they founded. Accepting that the audience is variegated means finding spaces within the stadia to accommodate all their different needs. As new stadia are built, their design should take the multi-faceted nature of the crowds that will fill them into sympathetic account.

If it does reach out to new constituencies, football has the potential to grow. At the moment, it has a particular problem with the laws of supply and demand. The small clubs are so economically hard-pressed by the boom that is benefiting the Premiership at their expense, that they lack the finances to fund an advertising campaign and loss-leader discount tickets to try to fill their half-empty stands. At the same time, at the top end of the Premiership, the stadia simply cannot accommodate the huge numbers chasing the precious few match tickets remaining after the season-ticket holders and corporate hospitality agents have taken their fill.

In the short term it must be in the interests of fans committed to their place in football's culture, to support and foster attempts to find other ways to follow their clubs which preserve and develop the tradition of live support. Opening up reserve games, youth and schoolboy matches to more than just the most committed of fans would be one option, turning these alternatives to first-team football into low-priced spectacles to generate new layers of support. The clubs that have experimented with this kind of endeavour, notably Leicester City, tell a powerful success story which is helping to bring new audiences into the ground.

Similarly, while pay-per-view on television will undoubtedly gain a profit-making momentum that will become impossible for the club chairmen to resist, it will at the same time further atomize and individualize our ability to watch the game. Beaming matches into local cinemas – the stalls and circles would be transformed into lookalike terraces, providing an opportunity for fans to sing, chant and wave banners – would be a low-tech way of at least making an effort to nurture the collective experience that is football. It would particularly appeal to young fans who don't have the money week in week out to attend live games. And while it may be second best to actually being there, it would be better than nothing.

Of course the big choice that football has to make is whether or not to face the future and make a long-term investment in vastly-increased stadia capacity that would be able to hold the rising numbers wanting to watch games live. The capital required, and the length of time that would be required to recoup these funds, suggest that the only viable strategy for securing such a future would be one founded on ensuring that the loyalty of the vastly-increased numbers required to fill the new stadia is secured by something easier to guarantee and perpetuate than success on the pitch.

To this end, the laws of the market – should the market be fans rather than TV and sponsorship contracts – might well force through the kinds of changes that will result in fans getting a far better deal from their clubs. In this admittedly optimistic scenario, the holistic approach referred to earlier would begin to unfold at the more enlightened clubs, and if successful, release the pressure for change elsewhere. Surely the football authorities should be

218

playing their part to help ensure this process starts before it is too late.

If this process did begin, women fans would move to at least the inside right position of football's front line for the future. We are a massive, untapped, but increasingly sympathetic audience, just waiting nervously to be asked to play ball. We are likely to respond far better to a club that thinks of all our needs – and not just to make the quickest possible buck out of those needs – than one that simply expects us to mimic the male traditions of old.

To honour the past by taking the best elements from it is something quite different to the resistance to all change that many masculine nostalgia trips into history are an excuse for. This opposition is fuelled by a male fondness – implicit and explicit – for a past where women were known for the supposedly submissive way in which they accepted their place in the great scheme of things. For men who are scared that women will soften the edges of the less attractive elements of fan culture, while having the independence and autonomy to make sure we can't be pushed around, the past is the only safe haven.

It is in all fans' potential interest to secure women's stake in the game by founding its position in the leisure industries of the new millennium on growing live support. It is sociologically, culturally and economically unrealistic to expect that this support will continue to be determined by simple ties of family connections and geography. And the questions remain: whose blood, whose geography? The peoples' game has in reality always been a sport for some people at the expense of others.

219

If the clubs are to risk their futures on attendances continuing to grow at a sufficient rate to make new stands and bigger stadia a realistic option, they are saying fans are here to stay, to co-exist alongside the satellite TV deals, the pay-per-view options and whatever cyberspace may yet have to offer.

This is a scenario that provides the opportunity for football to refashion its culture, to turn its back on a century or more of exclusivism and open itself out to a new populism. There's nothing necessarily wrong with 'making fans', and there's potentially plenty wrong with the self-satisfied assumption that both the businessmen who run football and many of the more defensively-minded fans share, that those who follow football are 'born not made'.

Turning the marketing, communications and promotional techniques of today to the task of reaching out and recruiting new live audiences could do much to both give the game the financial viability to fund the kind of stadia most fans would welcome and specifically address the women who have been kept out of the game for too long.

Our missionary position won't break the ties that once cemented the relationship between fan and club. But it will face up to the geographical and social mobility that means football simply cannot turn the clock back. Nor do we want to break the ties of blood, but we will challenge the notion that this is solely something passed on from father to son, man to boy. We will be ensuring that the daughters, girls and women get a look-in too.

**220**

Changing the game in this way might not turn the world upside down: it's not what we are setting out to do, this is football we're following, not netball. But it might just be as well for the men who continue to stand in our way to rue the words of one Oscar Wilde: 'Football is a game for rough girls, hardly suitable for delicate boys.'

# Index

**225**